A Bend
Willows *in the*

The Art of Making
Rustic Furniture

Paul Dolphin

FIFTH
HOUSE

D0521617

Cover and interior design by John Luckhurst / GDL
Photography by Paul Dolphin, Big Moon Rustic Furniture (www.bigmoonfurniture.com)
Illustrations by Toby Foord
All scans by St. Solo Computer Graphics (www.stsolo.com)

The publisher gratefully acknowledges the support of The Canada Council for the Arts
and the Department of Canadian Heritage. We acknowledge the financial support of the
Government of Canada through the Book Publishing Industry Development Program
for our publishing activities.

Printed in Canada by Transcontinental

02 03 04 05 06 / 5 4 3 2 1

First published in the United States in 2002 by

Fitzhenry & Whiteside
121 Harvard Avenue, Suite 2
Allston, MA
02134

National Library of Canada Cataloguing in Publication Data

Dolphin, Paul, 1963–
A bend in the willows

ISBN 1-894004-57-4
1. Wicker furniture. 2. Furniture making. 3. Country furniture.
I. Title.
TT197.7.D64 2002   684.1'04   C2002-910909-4

Fifth House Ltd.
A Fitzhenry & Whiteside Company
1511-1800 4 St. SW
Calgary, Alberta, Canada
T2S 2S5

1-800-387-9776
www.fitzhenry.ca

CONTENTS

Arbors or bowers frame entrances and provide support for climbing plants.

ACKNOWLEDGMENTS

This book is dedicated to the memory of Graham Greenshaw.

There are many people who must be thanked for helping to make this book a reality: the artisans I have met along the way who shared their craft with me, be it rustic furniture building or otherwise; my workshop students, who taught me how to teach; the staff at Big Moon Rustic Furniture, who weren't always thrilled at the prospect of posing for photographs; the staff at Fort Edmonton Park; everyone at Fifth House for their guidance and expertise; my father, who taught me his craft; and to Tina Mae for her patience, support, and love.

Children love a seat that is their size.

This ornate rocker is built with layers of bent willow.

PREFACE

It was a day like many others as I drove west to the foothills of the Rocky Mountains. I had made this trip to the forest many times during the years that I had been building rustic furniture. It was a typical cloudy morning in late September when the first signs of winter appear and a shiver runs through your body as you slowly begin to acclimatize to the hints of the cold season ahead.

I was taken by surprise when the weather report predicted the day's high temperature would remain below the freezing mark, and even more surprised when snow began to appear along the sides of the road. Somewhat unprepared, I nonetheless decided to carry on with my planned day of cutting wood. After a couple of hours of travel, I arrived at one of my favorite willow bogs.

Disembarking from my trusty, four-wheeled steed, I shivered as I pulled on my rubber boots and trekked into the bush. The forest was coated in ice, with a light dusting of snow. Apparently, Mother Nature was as unprepared for the drop in temperature as I was. From the path I could see a clearing in the distance, where a doe and fawn grazed in the tall grass, oblivious to my presence.

The woods are filled with fleeting wonders.

Within a few minutes I was busy with my wood-cutting, and my shivers turned to sweat as I felled large willow stocks with a handsaw. The gray serenity of the sheltered willow patch was suddenly shattered by the sun as it broke through the clouds and instantly raised the temperature the few degrees necessary to liberate the forest from winter's icy grip.

In that startling moment, the solid water was transformed into liquid and I was caught in the shower that fell from the treetops, soaking me instantly from head to rubber boots. Rather than get upset at this turn of events, I paused to enjoy the moment, and regarded my sopping garments as a small price to pay for the privilege of witnessing an instantaneous change in season.

Over the previous few years I had slowly come to the realization that my time spent as a lumberjack was my favorite part of building rustic furniture. What had begun as a difficult chore was now something I looked forward to. I finally understood that perhaps it was a longing to relate to Nature that had started my obsession with all things rustic.

It was a seminal moment; I experienced a transformation so profoundly subtle that it took my breath away. Within a few seconds winter had changed back into fall. I stood, soaking wet, in awe of Nature's diverse splendor. The forest had engulfed me, surrounded me, and treated me like any other creature who enters its majesty. All of these events brought me to the realization that I was now connected in the most humbling way to the natural environment, as I had wanted so many years before when I began my career as a underwoodsman.

I was amazed by my place in the world, and revelled in my own smallness. Mother Earth had shown me that like a deer I would come and go, leaving nothing for the annals of time to savor. I was filled, as I had been once before standing at the precipice of the Grand Canyon, with an overwhelming illustration of my insignificance. From this perspective, I was now able to truly appreciate the value of Nature: its diversity, randomness, and magical allure.

Rambling through the bush has granted me astonishing insights to an amazing world: beaver dams, bird nests, and spider webs built by living creatures and engineered to the highest possible standards, with an efficiency and simplicity that humans could never achieve. Some of the other joys of the woods include the smells, sounds, and sights of the forest, such as the unexpected joy of stumbling across a beautiful wildflower in full bloom, sighting a truly wild animal, or more exciting yet, the realization that a wild creature has spotted you.

I came to the world of building rustic furniture completely by accident. While working as a newspaper photographer, I chanced upon a bent willow chair at a botanical garden where I had been sent to take some pictures of a new butterfly exhibit. I thought the chair was curious; I had never seen anything like it. I took a few pictures of the chair and then thought no more about it.

Several years later I discovered a friend was making furniture in the same style. She taught me how to make the basic chair, and from there my hobby turned into an obsession and a livelihood.

I never planned to change careers; the joy and satisfaction of building things are a lot like the creativity of taking photographs, but I felt drawn to explore the woods. I was building chairs and driving down back roads. The more involved I got, the further into the woods I ventured.

There, I found the most complex, diverse, and awe-inspiring network of creatures and plants in a world that I knew existed, but hadn't bothered to explore since I was a child. My new work led me to a change in the way I approached life, and in that change I found a place between the raw materials provided by the Earth and the world we humans have fashioned. I simplified my life and work, and unwittingly found that by opening my eyes and mind to the possibilities inherent in Nature, each day has the potential to become a unique experience, full of learning.

CHAPTER ONE

DESIGN

I saw the integral role that design plays in our life plainly demonstrated by a five-year-old boy at a local fast-food restaurant. The boy was playing hopscotch on the two color floor tiles that led patrons down the hall to the restrooms. He had seen a random detail in the floor as a plaything. There was a designated play area with the visual impact of a sledgehammer only 20 feet away, yet he chose to enjoy this space. The boy was open to his environment, attentive to detail, and in tune with his surroundings.

Design is simultaneously both the easiest and most challenging part of any creative process. It starts with an idea or an experience and can take many different directions. Ideas for design come from all around us: the forest, the library, work by other artisans, even the normally uninspiring television.

A wise, not-so-old art teacher of mine always said it was impossible to steal another artist's idea; she insisted that no one could have a patent on inspiration. She felt that ideas could occur to more than one person and that perspective was the main factor in all expression. After many years of marking assigned work from her classes, she had never seen two students produce identical works.

With rustic construction, the diversity of Mother Nature and her materials ensures that every project will be unique. There are as many ways to use the different materials as there are variations in nature, with each

Patio screens create height and privacy in the garden.

Different materials have specific properties that can influence the overall design. This hotel reception desk uses a variety of woods to create a warm, welcoming impression.

2

wood providing properties that can be employed to advantage.

Start with an idea, borrowed or original, and decide which basic elements you will use. Who is the piece for? Where will it live? What is its main function? All these questions should be answered by the design.

No job should be too daunting to be attempted. Very seldom am I offered the opportunity to design a commission without parameters, and most times the client is involved in the creative process. Any artist with an appetite soon learns that no suggestion should be dismissed without consideration. You will be amazed at the things you learn by interpreting an idea that you otherwise may never have considered. Challenges are what make the creative process so rewarding.

I find that drawing a rough sketch that includes measurements helps to distill an idea. Using a tape measure, I rough out the size of the piece in the air, and then start working through the building process with a pencil, transferring the idea from the air to paper. After deciding on the type of wood I will use,

the basics of the frame, and the methods of joinery, I enhance the drawing and note any specific requirements.

The wood pieces that you cut will also influence the design of an individual piece, or even a whole set of furniture, often requiring that the plan be adjusted as the piece is built. Once I'm finished a project, I have a record that can be filed away, although often the paper is never looked at again. The important thing is that I was able to visualize and reference the idea and to work and rework the design before and during the building process.

Once you have a basic design, slight variations can be introduced to improve the performance or comfort of the design. This is a long-term process, so remember that Rome was not built in a day, and that each piece you build will be better than the last.

Building projects and using them are the best ways to test your design. It often takes several attempts at a project before an idea is successfully realized. Not every project will be a success from a design point of view. Design is a process, not an end in itself. Failures are a necessary part of learning a craft.

Left: A woven burlap seat provides a durable and comfortable seat for this dining chair.

Baskets can be designed to suit any purpose.

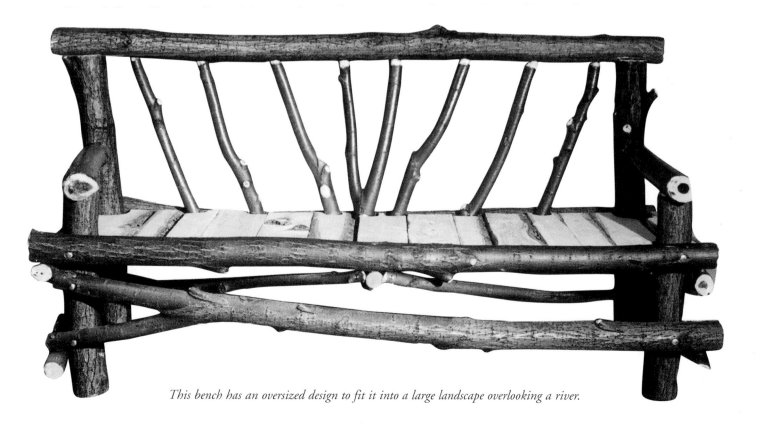

This bench has an oversized design to fit it into a large landscape overlooking a river.

Woodcutting and Design

Woodcutting is an essential part of the design process. I always cut with specific projects in mind, so I visit forest areas where I know the wood will have the specific properties I need for the job. Two important factors in choosing wood include: the size of the wood needed and whether or not it has to bend. The quality of soil, the lay of the land, and the moisture levels will contribute to the properties of wood. (See Chapter Three for more information on woodcutting.)

When I first started, I looked for long, straight pieces that would be easy to build with. I slowly began to appreciate the beauty of the curves and twists that plants use to grow toward the sun and the ways these shapes could be used to enhance the design of furniture. Sometimes a certain tree or the crook of a branch dictate an obvious use designed by Mother Nature. Make a point of wandering through the woods or looking down an unexplored road on every cutting trip—it is a very productive exercise that will inspire and hone your design skills.

Try using different materials to see how they perform throughout the building process, as well as over the course of time. I started working with willow, which grows in an infinite number of varieties. Instead of concentrating on a certain type of willow, I focused on the qualities I needed from the wood. I found the environment in which the plant was growing was more important to the wood's performance than whether it was species *Salix discolor* or species *Salix fluviatilis*.

Once I had experience with willow, I started to compare it to other woods like birch and alder, discovering that different types of wood give you a range of design options. Your choice of materials is crucial to the structural integrity of the piece, so find something that works and is plentiful. Soon the subtle differences in the wood will begin to appear of their own accord.

Willow in the Garden

The use of coppice woods or rustic woods in the garden has enjoyed a renewed popularity in recent years. The natural elements used in rustic furnishings and accessories easily and elegantly make the transition from exterior to interior. I became aware of using natural materials or unprocessed resources while working as a gardener on an estate in Wales. I have always had an acute interest in gardening, but being raised in North America I was accustomed to the symmetrical, highly organized yards of suburbia.

Materials such as stone and wood help to give interior design a natural feel.

Left: A trellis can be made in any size and with an infinite variety of designs.

This gate and lattice fence feature an inlaid door.

Tightly woven willow panels add some privacy to this yard.

Mortise and tenon construction makes this peeled willow bench, with a cedar seat, solid and stable.

An inlaid willow side table with a plant shelf.

The small church features a functioning bell in its tower.

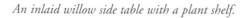

The British garden was a stark contrast to my perception of what was normal. The elements of the garden were allowed to grow wild and interact with each other—lawns were left shaggy, plantings were less organized, and generally the garden had a more unkempt look. Natural materials were used everywhere.

One of my daily tasks was to collect flowers for the manor house, and I used a woven willow basket to gather them. A willow broom was used to sweep the pavements throughout the pleasure gardens. Wheelbarrows and rakes were constructed out of natural materials, as were many of the other tools and the repair parts for the tools. Fences, shelters, and outbuildings had a simple, rustic style that blended back into the natural environment when they were aged and weathered.

I had the pleasure of watching some men thatch the roof of a cottage in a village on the estate. The skill and speed with which they worked was fascinating. They used local material that was gathered and delivered by one man, while two others built the roof.

In a week or so the roof was completely redone and the craftsmen moved on. Their craft, which was once a common skill, had become specialized and in great demand.

Almost anything can be constructed of natural elements, such as birdhouses, planters, chairs, tables, and benches, or even larger structures like bowers, arbors, fences, and patio screens.

Start with a simple project for a specific spot in the garden and go from there. I encourage people to start with a chair, then sit in their yard and imagine the place that they would like it to be. Use woods, metal, and stone to create texture and bulk in your garden. Arbors, fences, and gates create height. Incorporate living things into every area to introduce color. Finally, see how things age and weather, which techniques stand the test of time, and which ones need rethinking.

Clever design works as a cohesive group of elements, not as a single item. Create an environment that feels comfortable for you and is pleasing to the eye. A garden should be a place to relax and relate to the natural environment.

This birch and alder dining set has a linear design that stands in contrast to the broken tile tabletop.

8

Natural slate has a heavy, organic look that goes well with dark wood.

CHAPTER TWO

HISTORY OF RUSTIC FURNITURE

The story of rustic design is as old as the history of furniture itself. Certainly the first items we would call "furnishings" would have been fashioned out of simple natural materials, made with simple techniques, and used near the spot where the materials were gathered.

As people became more sophisticated, so too did the design and techniques used to make furniture. Rustic furniture evolved into a style that was associated with a rural existence. Rural society has always had a strong bond to the land, often employing natural materials out of necessity and practicality. As people moved away from a more direct reliance on the land and moved to the cities, life and furnishings became more refined. It was about the eighteenth century that rustic furniture as we know it began slowly moving from the home into the garden.

The word "rustic" is defined as: of the country, rural, uncultured. Despite this somewhat unflattering definition, rustic furnishings are used by every culture around the world and in all strata of society.

Europeans immigrating to the new world brought with them their traditions and culture which certainly included rustic furniture, but they had to adapt traditional techniques to work with local materials.

Upstate New York became a hotbed of furniture design and manufacturing. The Adirondack Chair is famous all over North America, recognizable to many people who can't even pronounce Adirondack. Artisans built rustic furniture in all parts of the country using the new materials they encountered in North America, enhancing and revitalizing the art form. American landscape architects embraced the design possibilities of the more natural materials.

Factories and farms dedicated to producing rustic furnishings stretched down the east coast to Florida and over into the Midwest. Rustic furniture for cottages and summer homes was produced to meet the demands of the exploding population and rising affluence of this new society. While eastern North America built factories and metropolises, people continued to settle the West throughout the nineteenth century. In western North America, rustic furnishings were associated with the cowboy or ranching lifestyle, where designs evolved in more of a utilitarian manner. This furniture was made up of simple objects that could withstand the ravages of the weather.

Over the years rustic furniture has enjoyed revivals of popularity, most often during times of uncertainty or rapid progress. This longing for a simpler life is neither new nor incomprehensible—it has affected humanity ever since survival was replaced with work. Whenever the pace of life or societal change becomes excessive, it is natural to look to the past with a sense of longing for lost simplicity, fueled by a belief that past times were more honest and straightforward than the complicated life of today.

In reality, few of us would have been able to handle the workload and character that immigration and life in a new land demanded. It is, however, easy to identify with the spirit of settlers who came to carve out a new and better life; their values included hard work, freedom, stewardship of the land, and respect for the power and beauty of nature.

Two Worlds Collide

Here is a glimpse of how far we've come over the past 250 years: the first Europeans to arrive in western Canada, where I now live, were fur traders who first made contact with the Native peoples. For thousands of years these people had reaped the benefits of the rich forests and grasslands and at regular times of the year the communities would gather at points along the rivers to trade and socialize. When the first Europeans arrived in the 1700s, they established a prosperous fur trade that used the river system to transport trade goods to the West and furs to the East to feed Europe's insatiable desire for beaver pelt hats.

Fort Edmonton was part of the Hudson's Bay Company's system of fur-trading posts. (Fort Edmonton Park)

The two principal companies, The Hudson's Bay Company and The North West Company, created a series of trading posts that stretched across Canada's west and north. The Natives helped the Europeans adjust to life on the frontier by guiding and teaching them, and by trading with them. Their knowledge about the environment, the weather, and the numerous natural resources was invaluable to the newcomers.

Beaver pelts and other furs were transported in York boats, which were built and repaired at the inland forts. The workhorses of the trading system, these wooden boats were similar to a large canoe, and freighted furs along rivers and lakes to York Factory, which was situated on Hudson Bay, where the furs were loaded onto ships that took them to England. The York boats were the semi-trailers of their day, but they were powered by paddlers using raw human strength. Each had a crew of eight to ten men, depending on their size: one bowsman, six middlemen (or oarsmen), and one steersman, as well as the occasional passenger. On the return trip from York Factory the boats were laden with tools, foodstuffs, and a variety of other items to supply the forts and trade with the

Native peoples for their furs. (The forts were the precursor to settlement in the West, but yielding to pressures to settle the prairies, the Hudson's Bay Company sold its territories to the government of Canada in 1870.)

The remoteness and the long winters, a time when goods could not be moved, meant that each fort had to be self-sufficient. It was a place isolated from all modern conveniences, where every resource had to be located, harvested, and refined on site or shipped in from the outside world at great expenditure of time, labor, and money.

The fur-trading posts varied in size, housing a variety of men and their families. Administrators, clerks, carpenters, boat builders, blacksmiths, general laborers and boatmen (or "crew" as the company referred to them), along with their wives and children all lived and worked together to maintain and improve the fort.

A journal of daily activities from Fort Edmonton provides a telling insight into daily life 150 years ago. A wide variety of activities were necessary to support the community. Crews of men were sent to the forest for many different tasks: to cut spruce and pine timbers; to collect birch for making dog sleighs; to gather pine roots to carve into parts for the boats; and to collect pine pitch to use for sealing seams in canoes. Men were also dispatched on hunting and fishing excursions or to cut ice from the river. Within the confines of the fort, there were guns and traps to repair, buildings to mud, livestock to tend, and a seemingly inexhaustible supply of other maintenance jobs. The women's activities were not recorded in the post journal because they were not officially engaged by the company, but they would have been busy managing gardens, harvesting and preserving crops, cooking, and baking bread in an outdoor oven, as well as caring for and educating the children.

Carpenters built buildings, furniture, and vehicles, as well as maintaining the company's fleet of boats, all done using a wide variety of hand tools. The cut timbers were processed in different manners, depending on their end use. Rough deals (or logs) were squared with a broad ax or adze and then the rounded side was removed using a hewing ax. Large timbers could then be cut into planks using a pit saw. This was a two-story saw operated by two men. One stood above the log on a platform, with the log lying between his feet, and the

Furniture on the frontier reflected the temporary lifestyle of the pioneers. (Fort Edmonton Park)

other stood below the log, in a pit. The job of the top sawman was to lift and guide the blade of the two-handled saw as it cut down the length of the log. The pitman's job was to pull hard on the saw's downward cutting stroke and oil the blade with a bit of linseed oil on each upward stroke. The plank could then be further smoothed and refined using smaller saws, axes, and planes. An awl was used to pre-drill nail holes; gimlets, augers, and bitstock were used to drill holes. Chisels, gouges, mallets, and hammers in many shapes and sizes filled the shelves of the workshop.

There were specialty tools back then, too. A froe was used to split wood for shingles, and a cooper's adze was a curved ax used to make staves for wooden barrels. The various trades worked together to design a utilitarian environment that was efficient as well as comfortable. The blacksmith's shop produced tools, hardware, and horseshoes while still maintaining and repairing equipment.

Space was at a premium in the early years of the settlements, but as time went on the standard of living in the forts rose. Lodgings and amenities, including furniture, were assigned according to a person's place in the fort's pecking order.

Bachelor quarters were a barrack-style hall where men slept and ate. It was sparsely furnished with a few crude benches and tables, with pallet beds that were fashioned out of whole logs. Married men and their families had slightly more private quarters, though up to three families would share a chamber that had a higher level of comfort, including a fireplace for cooking. Although modest, these communal dwellings had a bit of room for a comfortable chair or cradles for the infants.

The senior officers of the Hudson's Bay Company

As life became more permanent on the frontier, furniture design became more intricate. (Fort Edmonton Park)

11

Many early settlers to North America started from nothing and had to use the resources at hand to build a life.
(Fort Edmonton Park)

had separate apartments, and the chief factor, or general manager of the district, had his headquarters in prestigious living quarters—often a separate house. Fort Edmonton's Big House, a massive log building, was furnished in a simple, straightforward style graced with the odd antiquity which had also made the long journey from the old country.

Willow and birch were commonly used to make chairs, stools, and side tables. Pine and spruce were generally used to make all kinds of larger furnishings. Tables, benches, and beds were padded with straw or dried moss covered with buffalo hide. Plank wood was used to make shelving and simple boxes for storage. A visitor to Fort Edmonton in 1841 described the quarters provided as "exceedingly comfortable."

The visitor would have enjoyed willow and birch furniture similar to the furniture still being produced by artisans today. These simple designs have not changed much over time. More prestigious quarters in the fort would have had more ornate furnishings, but

simple, functional design was a consistent factor throughout the range of furniture at the fort, and this same sense of design and style can be achieved today, using the same materials as our ancestors. This glimpse into the past illustrates what could be done then with hand tools and local resources. It was a life very different from today—imagine not having electricity and all the conveniences it brings. There were no quick fixes from the local hardware store—ingenuity, resourcefulness, industry, and discipline were the character traits needed to prosper under these conditions.

These early pioneers did succeed, and forged a path for all of us who have followed and are now lucky enough to live in this bountiful part of the world. We should be careful to acknowledge that the path they took led through the natural world. If you look with open eyes, you too can find the same path and walk a few miles down that road. It leads to an amazing place—one that we must learn to respect and preserve, for many more will follow the path after us.

CHAPTER THREE

COLLECTING MATERIALS

Wood is probably the most useful and adaptable renewable resource on Earth; it is found everywhere people live. A staple of human existence, trees have long been employed not only to make life livable, but more enjoyable, too.

There are many ways of using plants: for shelter, as an energy source, to make paper, dyes, syrups, and medicines. All parts of trees can be refined and processed into an almost limitless number of products. The wood alone has amazing qualities that allow it to be cut, carved, and joined to create almost any shape.

Rustic construction differs from more common techniques in that many of the materials are acquired in a raw form or taken directly from the forest. Wood and other basic elements like stone, rock, and glass can be combined with milled lumber and simple hardware

to create furniture that maintains a link to the natural world. Perhaps surprisingly, it also requires little in the way of tools and skill to successfully build a piece of furniture.

Working with wood is a satisfying way to spend your time. The wood is part of the natural world, with rustic construction taking you one step further toward that idyllic world because you collect your own wood directly at the source.

I have witnessed many times the pride students feel at completing their first chair. They have a satisfied feeling of accomplishment, something I still feel myself when viewing one of my completed projects. In rustic construction, the link to the wood's origin can add immeasurably to that feeling of satisfaction.

Coppice wood, drift wood, dead standing timber,

A snow-covered marsh contains lots of willow benders. Frozen winter conditions allow easy access to wetlands.

The sheltered quiet of a willow bog.

and live timber are found abundantly in nature. Most rustic materials can be acquired with little negative impact on the Earth, simply by choosing selectively and being respectful toward the environment.

Coppice is an old English word that refers to the new undergrowth of hardwood trees regularly harvested for use in gardens or as a household resource. Collecting coppice wood was considered a necessary part of farm management. Furniture, home accessories, garden structures, tools, and containers were all made using the collected undergrowth.

Willow is not a coppice wood by definition because it grows as a bush or as a single plant. It does, however, behave similarly to coppice wood and has evolved into the bent furniture wood of choice in North America due to its flexibility and availability.

Willow has a long and culturally important history. The Celts revered willow as a sacred wood and European Gypsies believed it had great powers of fertility. The ancient Romans were aware of the medicinal properties of salicylic acid, the active ingredient in Aspirin, which is contained in the bark of willow trees.

Willow grows all over the planet in many different forms. As a plant that easily hybridizes and adapts, willow propagates abundantly wherever there is a high water table, rich soil, and plenty of sunlight.

Finding the right type of willow is a skill that becomes easier with experience, but the only way to get that experience is to head out and see what you can find. In hindsight, my first few forays into woodcutting were quite disastrous. I had trouble telling a poplar from a willow and had no idea where to look for the wood I needed. As a result, I spent countless hours driving farm roads, searching the ditches for straight willow bushes. Eventually, I found my way to the woods.

As time went by, it became easier to distinguish different species and different varieties. You should never discount any wood as a source; instead, recognize that some types will be easier to work with than others, some will weather better, and some will look better. But any abundant source of wood should be considered. For example, I once built a two-story, "Little House on the Prairies" playhouse using lumber salvaged from unwanted shipping pallets. There was a lot of nail pulling and a little head scratching involved, but the finished product never divulged the secret. Diversity of plant life is the key to rustic furniture design, so find a plentiful source of wood in your region and start experimenting.

In North American society, wood is constantly wasted or seen as having no value in the "time is money" economy. Sources of salvaged and recycled wood are easy to find without ever leaving the city. Bulldozing down trees is the quickest way to ready land for construction and development, so check the outskirts of any town or city and chances are there will be plenty of trees on death row. City forestry crews and private tree-cutting companies are always open to lightening their workload by sharing the trees they cut—you're saving them the trouble of "disposing" of the wood.

In rural areas, power and phone lines are continually cleared of brush, which leaves ditches full of fast-growing species that like a steady supply of water. Stay a few steps ahead of the brush-cutting crews and you'll have plenty of material.

Be mindful of private property and public land surrounding the area where you've chosen to cut wood.

Willow bushes most often have canoe-shaped leaves.

A birch grove in mid-summer.

Nobody likes to see someone cutting down that tree that grandpa planted way back when. Rather than ticking off its citizens, most local governments have set aside public land for cutting firewood, where you can cut your wood in peace. Contact the forestry or environmental department to check the regulations concerning cutting in these areas.

I prefer to work mainly with willow bushes. In my neck of the woods, willow grows everywhere and in a wide variety of sizes. As the wood dries it becomes very hard and strong, with little shrinkage. I also work with birch, alder, mountain ash, and pine, as well as an assortment of other woods, but willow remains my main material. Besides its obvious attributes for furniture construction, it is full of surprising crooks and bends to keep the artist and designer in you happy.

Although you don't need to be an expert on the different types of willow in North America, a bit of information will go a long way. Because the plant easily propagates hybrids, searching for just the right plants to cut can be confusing, but in my experience, the plant species is only as important as where the plant is growing. A constant and plentiful water supply is essential to fast, straight growth and good flexibility. Another trait to watch for is how well the wood weath-

ers. Some species of willow hold up better than others; try a few different varieties to see which does the best.

You can cut wood at any time of year and use it right away. If you are building a project that requires bending or uses the overlap method of joinery, fresh wood will work best. It is a good idea to let the wood season for a few days to reduce the moisture level and make the bark less susceptible to injury. Wood that is cut during the growing season will be more fragile because of the high moisture level in the layer of wood growing just under the bark.

It is best to cut wood in the winter for many reasons. First, the wood will still be pliable, but with the sap down in the roots, the bark will be better sealed and less likely to peel during construction and over the course of time. Second, without leaves it is much easier to select the wood you want. Third, because the ground is frozen when you are cutting, it is much easier to access the stand of trees, which usually grows in damp conditions. The fourth good reason is that cutting wood is hard, hot work, so the winter weather can make the experience much more pleasant. Finally, the absence of mosquitoes and other stinging insects is a bonus that should not be understated.

A small bow saw and a pair of large pruning shears is all that is required to fell trees.

Collect a little more wood than you estimate you will need, and be sure to select the best materials you can find.

16

Always wear rubber boots and eye protection. As you move through to collect it, the willow can hurt you by forcefully snapping back into place. Gloves are also essential equipment to prevent badly scratched hands. As far as tools go, all you need are a large and small pair of clippers, a bow saw, and some rope to bundle the wood for easy handling.

Look for willow bushes with a ready supply of water. You shouldn't have to venture too far from the roadside to collect what you need; this will also make it easier to haul the wood back to your vehicle. Cut and bend the willow right on site, and if it doesn't bend well, move on until you find wood that does what you want. Be selective: the better the willow bends, the easier the construction will be later.

Keep in mind that you don't need the whole forest to build a chair; thirty benders and four or five framing pieces will be plenty. Always cut a little more than you think you will need, because pieces break or get damaged, or don't look quite as straight at home as they did in the forest. The leftover pieces can be allowed to dry and used later in different types of projects.

If you have access to land with willow growing on it, consider trying to cultivate a willow patch to suit your specific needs. The easiest way to do this is to find a few varieties of willow that you like to work with and cut off several stalks. Cut these pieces into 8-inch lengths and plant them a few feet apart in moist soil, with the top 4 inches of the stalk exposed. Another transplanting method is to dig up some of the roots of the plant you wish to grow and bury 2-inch sections of them a few inches below the surface of the soil.

The willow should grow easily, and within a year start to send out lots of shoots. Trim the bushes, encouraging the straightest shoots to grow. In a few years you will have a steady supply of good bending material.

Storing Wood

Storing the wood is an important consideration. Keeping willow "fresh" requires reducing the air circulation around the wood and keeping it cool. Tie willow logs and benders in tight bundles and store them in a cool, dark place, such as a concrete basement floor. If you don't have room to store them indoors, place the ends of the whole bundle in a bucket of water that is placed at the base of a tree. String rope around the bundle and the tree to hold the bundle upright and steady.

Winter storage is easy. Cut a bunch of wood in the fall, wrap the bundles in a tarp, and allow them to freeze. Then just thaw and use them as necessary.

When your goal is to season or dry the wood, take the opposite approach. The wood must have good air circulation under dry conditions. The best situation is to have wood stored inside where it has no exposure to undue moisture and, most important, ultraviolet radiation. Cut the wood into standard-sized pieces and store them either leaning upright or lying on shelves so that both ends have good air movement around them.

If you have to store wood outdoors, be careful to keep it well sheltered. Don't find yourself suffering from "woodpile syndrome," in which wood gets moist and bugs move in. Once this happens, the wood is no longer usable for construction.

Safety

Safety in and around wood and the places you find it should be your first concern when out cutting wood. Felling trees has inherent dangers. With smaller timbers the concern is cutting yourself or poking your eye out—yes, your mother has already warned you about this, so listen up.

Larger timbers can do major damage and should be approached with great respect. I hesitate to cut any trees more than 4 inches in diameter unless I have someone to act as a spotter. Take time to determine which way a tree is going to fall, and always have an escape route planned on the chance that something unexpected happens. Once it is clear the tree is falling, move away from the area quickly and carefully.

The forest can be a dangerous place, where even the terrain can cause you to twist an ankle or worse. Always bring someone with you just in case of emergency, but if you must go alone, let someone know where you are going and what time you expect to be back.

The animals you will encounter in the woods are also a consideration. Remember that you are invading their home and that they should be given a wide berth. Although I don't have any snakes or alligators to worry about, where I live, snakes are a very real worry for many areas of North America, especially in the types of swampy terrain where willow grows. In my area, large mammals are the concern, and I have been lucky enough to see moose, deer, elk, wolves, bears, and even cougars while cutting wood. I say lucky, because I saw them from a distance and did not have to confront them. Tread lightly and deliberately, making lots of noise as you go, and chances are you'll be the last to know you have been near a wild animal.

Framing material and a bundle of benders ready to be hauled to town.

CHAPTER FOUR

TECHNIQUES

The design of any piece of furniture depends on many factors. Some consideration must be given to the structural requirements, the wood that will be used, and the type of joinery that will be employed. Plus, the aesthetics of the piece are also worthy of significant advance planning.

This chapter is a reference for planning your project construction and for problem-solving along the way. The techniques described here provide the basics of constructing rustic furniture. They are skills you will use over and over again. And, as you develop as an artisan, you will probably have a few paragraphs to add to this chapter yourself. Techniques born of necessity and your own inventiveness will almost certainly be the most valuable tricks in your toolbox.

Tools

The tools that are employed in building are as important as the techniques. The basic tools required to start building rustic projects are simple hand tools, many of which you may already have. Basically, you need to be able to cut and join wood, which requires a saw, a hammer, a drill, a good sharp knife, and a couple of pairs of pruning shears.

The pruning shears are used for cutting and trimming small pieces of wood. You will need both a single hand pair for fine, precise work and the larger version

The basic tools you need to get started.

for serious cutting. Use the type of shears that have a blade and an anvil (meaning that only one blade is pushing through the wood until it rests against the fixed anvil). This type of system cuts cleaner than the scissors-type tool, which is mainly used for cutting flowers.

The knife I use is a utility knife. I have tried a variety of blades and always return to this simple device. Cutting green wood dulls a blade very quickly, so the ease of replacing blades in this kind of knife allows you to always have a sharp cutting edge.

A bow saw works best for cutting the larger frame pieces. They come in several sizes; the smaller saws can give you an advantage in the tight spots you will encounter while collecting wood. Again, a supply of replacement blades will improve the ability of the saw to cut efficiently.

A hammer is a hammer is a hammer. Find one that fits in your hand and start swinging it.

With these simple tools, you should be able to handle most projects.

Keeping your cutting tools sharp is extremely important for both the fresh wood and your own sanity—dull tools will tear and damage the bark and make your cutting trip an aggravating wrestling match. The most expensive pair of pruning shears that is dull won't work half as well as an inexpensive pair that is regularly sharpened.

I sharpen most of my own tools myself, but do have them professionally sharpened if they are tricky to hone or if the blade has sustained damage that is beyond my ability to repair.

The choice of tools for any craftsperson is a personal one. All trades have standard tools that are used on a daily basis; add some specialty tools to this list and you'll have a full toolbox. An experienced craftsman gave me some good advice early on: "Always buy the best tools you can afford at the time, and the tools used most often should be of the highest quality."

I prefer hand tools for most tasks, although for some repetitive jobs pneumatic or air-nailing equipment is very handy. Although fast, the air-nailer will never have the accuracy of a nail hammered by hand. All hand-built projects should be manually fastened, both for strength and aesthetic appeal.

As you move into more complex projects, you'll require more sophisticated tools. The projects selected for this book require no more than the basic tools, although sometimes you will see us using more sophisticated versions of the basic tools.

"You can't have too many drills" is what I was once told by an old carpenter. It was many years later, in the midst of the chaos of a big job, that his advice finally made sense to me. The right tools will make the job easier and quicker, but not having a certain tool should never stop you from attempting a project. Do the best you can with the resources you have. It also makes for good stories you can tell your grandchildren.

Finally, always remember the first rule of tools: "The most important tool is the one you keep inside your head."

Whittling

The skill that should be mastered first by a rustic builder is whittling. There are several good reasons to whittle your logs: it gives the piece a more finished appearance; it cleans up the ragged ends left by the saw blade and helps to seal the bark; finally, it is the best way to deal with all the branches that must be trimmed. Whittling is also often employed to cut notches and trim a tenon (a peg).

A sharp knife is the key to successful whittling. I use a standard utility knife, and replace the blade often. Hold the knife inside a fist in your dominant hand. Place the edge of the blade just behind the branch stub, then anchor your other hand to the underside of the log and use the thumb of that hand to help push the blade through the wood. It will feel awkward at first, but by using both hands you will have much more control and strength. Make several light passes around a stub, rather than trying to remove it with one cut. Always cut up and away from yourself and you will have fewer accidents.

To whittle the end of a log, stand the log up vertically and hold it near the top. Place the blade at a 45-degree angle to the log and push the blade through the wood. It should make a crescent-shaped cut in the log. Start your next cut inside the last cut and continue making cuts around the edge of the log. The clean,

Using both hands to whittle gives you a lot more control, and ensures both wood and whittler emerge unscathed.

Whittling the ends of the log seals the bark and gives it a cleaner appearance.

sharp cut left by the knife will help the bark to heal nicely as it dries and shrinks down against the wood.

It won't take too long before you'll get a hankerin' to light your corn-cob pipe and do a little whistlin', while you're whittlin'.

Nails vs. Screws

There is a great debate among rustic furniture builders about the best way to fasten joints. Some nail them, others use pneumatic fasteners, and still others swear by screws. I have tried all these methods, and found that each works well for specific applications.

My overall preference is to use nails, because if used correctly, they will perform as well as any other method. They also are a lot less noticeable than screws and over time will blend in with the wood.

I usually use a combination of different nails, my favorite being galvanized finishing nails and galvanized casing nails. A casing nail has a larger, more tapered

19

head than a finishing nail and tends to hold things together better. The galvanized nail is protected against rusting and has a rough surface that allows it to fit snugly in a pre-drilled channel. A traditional common or penny nail will work fine, too, but I don't like the look of the large head. Some builders swear by spiral nails, which hold things together nicely, but are difficult to remove if you make a mistake.

Screws seem like the obvious choice for ease of use and for providing a good hold, but they can be problematic when working with green wood. From an aesthetic point of view the size and shine of wood screws also leaves a bit to be desired, especially when the screws are used with a finishing washer, which is necessary when building with green wood. The washer increases the surface area of the head and makes it more effective in pulling two pieces of wood together. The fins on a screw can also crack green wood, which shrinks as it dries.

I use wood screws often because they do have their place, but usually only on big projects or in applications where dry wood is used.

There are ways of minimizing the visual impact of screws, such as painting them a dark color to help camouflage them or, in mortise and tenon construction, countersinking the screws into the log and hiding them with a wooden plug. You will probably figure out a few tricks of your own once you have some experience with rustic furniture.

Pneumatic fasteners shoot nails or staples into the wood with a jet of air. They are quick and easy to use and require no pre-drilling. For this tool, I prefer staples over nails because the staples seem to have more strength and with two tines they hold better. Keep in mind that the time saved with these tools does come at a price—the nails are of a smaller gauge than standard nails of the same length, so they have less strength. The pneumatic fasteners also are less accurate than pre-drilling and nailing. They split the wood more often and can deflect off other nails, causing damage as the nail exits the wood.

Pneumatic nail guns work well for specific, small jobs, but even in these applications, real nails should be used to reinforce the air nails.

Pre-drilling

Pre-drilling a channel for the nail or screw to follow is the most important technique in rustic furniture construction. The most obvious benefit of pre-drilling is that the position and direction of the nail can be determined in advance. Trying to aim a nail into two round logs is difficult. The pre-drilled channel guides the nail into the final position and lessens the impact of the construction on the piece of furniture. Pre-drilling your nail channels also significantly reduces the chance that a log will split.

How deep to pre-drill the channels depends on the situation. With large nails the channel can be the same length as the nail, but small nails used to fasten little pieces need to bite into an anchor piece, so in these cases the nail channel should be much shorter than the nail.

Pre-drilling creates a channel to guide a nail into the desired position.

The relationship between the size of the nail shaft and the size of the drill-bit shaft that you use to pre-drill the nail channel is also very important. The drill-bit shaft should be slightly smaller in diameter than the nail so that the nail will fit tightly into the channel.

In some situations, the drill bit should have a larger diameter than the nail. For example, when green wood is used, particularly thin pieces that are nailed across the grain, like in the case of seat slats, it makes sense to leave room for the wood to shrink around the nail without cracking. In this application, use a nail that has a head large enough to hold the piece in place while it dries. With time the wood will shrink around the nails, tightening each joint. The heads of some nails will emerge from the wood due to the shrinkage and will need a final tap with the hammer.

Dulling the Nail Points

This old carpenter's trick is a valuable technique that is commonly used in finishing carpentry to avoid splitting small pieces of wood. A nail with a dulled point will be less likely to find its way between two wood fibers and cause the wood to split. This technique is often used when a nail has to be driven in near the end of a log or nailed in at a severe angle.

Dulling the head of the nail makes it less likely to split a piece of wood.

Double Nailing or Cross Nailing

Double nailing involves driving two nails in at opposing angles so that they cross paths. With the two nails inserted in this manner, it is difficult for the pieces to come apart.

When using this technique, the nails don't have to be at a particular angle or touch each other to be effective. Pre-drilling the nail channels is essential to the success of double nailing, because the likelihood that you will contact the first nail is high. If the nails do meet, try hammering lightly until the second nail finds its way past the first one.

Two nails inserted at angles to each other will hold pieces firmly in place.

Bending Wood

Bending wood is one of the great joys of rustic construction, when finding the perfect pieces for bending can be more exciting than actually building with them.

Many types of coppice wood can be bent or shaped. Willow ranks as one of the best bending woods, and even dry willow retains a liberal amount of flex and can be shaped into gentle curves. But the best bending results are always obtained using green or fresh wood.

A good piece of willow will bend easily into a curve, but the curve may not be even because of the taper of the piece. To get a more even curve, I usually bend the piece across my knee. I start with my hands shoulder-width apart and one leg raised on a stool or bench and bent at 90 degrees. I then rest the bender just under my kneecap and apply even pressure to the piece of wood with my hands, making a slight indentation every 5 inches or so, working from the thick end to thin and back again.

Be careful not to apply too much pressure or you may break the piece of wood—the goal is to shape the piece gently into an even curve. Bear in mind that the willow we use most commonly grows in a bush, and so

Bending and shaping wood requires patience and a gentle touch.

it competes for sunlight with other shoots and usually has a predisposed bend. Follow this bend as you shape your pieces.

If you have trouble curving a bender across your knee, bend the piece under your foot. If you do this, be even more careful not to apply too much force and break the piece. I find that I don't have quite the same fineness of feel when I am bending with my foot. I only bend under my foot when I am working with thicker pieces, and then bend them again along my knee just to make sure they have the suppleness required.

Nailing Benders Together

To make bent willow furniture, you will often need to nail several bent pieces together, most commonly when you are building the arms or back of a bent willow piece. Being able to do this effectively will make all your projects look better and age more gracefully. These bent pieces dry in a matter of a few weeks, and once dry, the willows hold their shape, so keeping the benders in position during the drying time is crucial.

Balancing curves in bent furnishings relies on a balanced construction approach. Select benders with similar properties and split up your resources evenly. For example, in the case of making a chair, always select two bending pieces at a time, one for each side of the chair. To keep the stresses on the frame equal throughout the building process, go from one side to the other when attaching your pieces. For the back curve, alternate from which side you start bending the thick end. If you use pieces of similar diameter, the curves will balance themselves out.

Finding a good fit before nailing is the real secret to achieving beautiful furniture. If you are lucky enough to be using arrow-straight pieces you won't have many problems, but if you are using less than perfect benders, a few pointers will come in handy.

I always use pieces that are longer than I need. This allows me to fit the new bender along the bender it will be anchored to, and I can match the best section of the new bender to the contours of its mate.

Nail the benders together, working from the thick end to the thin end, joining them in places where they come together naturally. If you have a spot that is forcing itself apart, try double nailing it. Often, the problem is a protrusion between the two benders that will not allow them to sit together comfortably. This is easily fixed by trimming any bumps that are causing the two pieces to fit awkwardly. When pre-drilling the nail channel, be careful not to drill too deeply—the nail should bite solidly into the anchor bender and hold its position.

Time spent pre-fitting and preparing the benders is well invested, and it will make the construction experience less stressful for both yourself and the piece of furniture.

Weaving Willow

Weaving wood is a satisfying process; the form is slowly filled, evolving into a finished product that is both distinctive and beautiful. "Wattle weaving" is the name most commonly used for this style of filling a surface with pieces that are woven through supports attached to the framework.

From fencing to basketry, pieces of any thickness can be woven with good results. The key is setting

Weaving wood can produce beautiful results.

your support pieces far enough apart to give you room to weave, and close enough together to give the structure stability.

The pieces to be woven must first be limbered up so that they will be able to be shaped easily (see the "Bending Wood" section above). Alternating the starting point from side to side will ensure that the weave is even and square. Finally, choosing the pieces carefully is the most important factor in achieving a balanced, aesthetically pleasing result.

A properly constructed weave will hold its shape by itself, but a few discreetly placed nails will help keep the pieces in position while the wood dries. I prefer using wood that has had a chance to dry a little before use, because the bark of partially dried wood is less

Ensure that end pieces fit well before nailing them together.

susceptible to injury. The best-case scenario is a woven project that is completed in stages, because the wood will have time to shrink and you will have time to make adjustments for the best fit.

Peeling Wood

Peeling logs produces wood that is as beautiful to touch as it is to look at. Taking the bark off trees is also fun, but can become addictive, so be careful. Woods are best peeled in the spring and summer when the plant is actively growing—the wetter the climatic conditions, the sweeter the peel. Because a new layer of cells is reproducing just under the bark, you can easily peel the wood and uncover a smooth surface that requires little sanding.

Use a chisel to separate the bark from the first layer of wood and pull the bark off. To make your life easier, remove the bark in strips, just like shucking a cob of corn. Peel the wood as soon as possible after cutting, otherwise the tannin in the bark will begin to stain the wood. Then store the logs upright in a place with good air circulation for quick drying—wood left in damp conditions can mildew. In just a month or two, the wood will be dry enough to work with.

Peeling wood out of season is a real chore. Depending on the moisture level of the wood, it can be very laborious. If you must peel logs when the plant is not growing, try stripping bark as you would in summer. If that fails, use a utility knife to peel the main bark as you would a potato. Then scrape the wood, dragging the edge of the blade back toward yourself to remove the remnants of the first layer of wood. You must let the wood dry before sanding can commence.

Peeling Birch Bark

The bark of birch trees has long been used for a variety of applications. It is very durable and versatile material and can be peeled easily. The bark should be peeled while the tree is actively growing.

To peel off the bark, simply cut through the first layer of bark with a utility knife and slowly separate the bark from the under layers of wood. Then use a putty knife or a thin wedge of wood to separate the bark by slowly pulling it away from the log. With practice you should be able to peel large sheets of the bark intact.

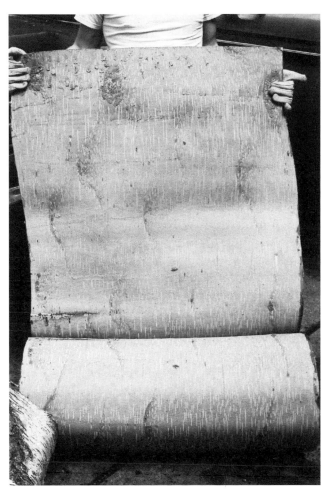

Birch bark is a durable and easy-to-use material.

Birch bark can be dried under a plywood sheet that is weighted to keep the bark flat, or by stretching the sheets in a frame where air can circulate around it and speed the drying process. The sheets will curl if left to dry without support. If you intend to shape the bark, or to attach it to a frame, do it soon after the bark is peeled.

Birch bark can be stained, which increases your design options, especially when using it as a veneer.

Make sure that the rest of the tree is cut and used. Trees that are peeled and left standing will eventually die and become unstable, causing a potential hazard to the forest population.

Overlapping Joinery

The simple style of overlapping joinery is used in many rustic projects to construct the frame. It requires fewer tools and less know-how than more complicated types of joinery, yet if built properly, this type of frame will serve many purposes well. Several of the plans in this book use this overlapping style, and by building different projects, you will learn how to adapt this frame for various applications.

In the overlapping style of joinery, pieces are joined together and then the joints are reinforced by nailing

Overlap joinery is a simple system that requires few tools.

the overlapping ends. These overlaps distribute the weight that the piece of furniture will bear. The frame is also braced where necessary to ensure that it is solid. Pay close attention to the frame, because it is the backbone of any project.

Mortise and Tenon Frames

The other common type of joinery for making frames is the mortise and tenon method. In this style, a tenon (or peg) is cut on the ends of rails and crossbeams and fit into a mortise (or hole) drilled into the vertical legs of the frame. In the simplest form of this style, the pegs extend right through to the outside of the logs. This book advocates a version that is more compli-

Paddle bits have a large cutting surface that works well on rough surfaces.

cated, solid, and aesthetically pleasing. A mortise and tenon frame will have a much cleaner final appearance than the overlapping-style frame. It requires less material, while also allowing you to make use of more of the frame's surface area.

The best results come with dry wood, where shrinkage has already occurred, so joints will have a tendency to stay put. Green wood can be used, and shrinkage will not be a concern if both elements of the joint shrink equally, but this isn't always the case. A further risk is that the glue will not set up properly if the wood is too moist. Green wood also dulls cutting edges quickly, and requires more effort from the builder. Once you use dry wood, its advantage over uncured wood will become clear.

Making a Mortise

The mortises are made by simply drilling a hole. A paddle drill bit works well to cut through the bark and make a clean hole in the wood. A drill press helps to make the mortise nice and straight, and also saves elbow grease.

Use dry wood for best results with mortise and tenon joinery.

Making a Tenon

The tenon (or peg) is cut to fit into the mortise. Once you have a good fit, the joint is glued and allowed to dry.

Hand-cut tenons can be made to any size. Inscribe the diameter of the tenon on the center of the end of the log with the same drill bit you used to make the mortise. Paddle bits work best because they have a blade that defines a groove around the outside of the cutting edge. Next, use a chisel to cut a line around

Getting mortises straight takes a little practice.

Cut tenons with a special tool available at wood-working stores.

the outside of the log a couple of inches from the end, then split away the excess material from the end of the log until you are close to the final tenon diameter required. Start trying to fit the tenon into the mortise, whittling with a knife until the proper diameter is attained.

Another method of making tenons is to use a hole saw to cut the tenon into the end of a log; the wood remaining between the incision and the edge of the log is then cut away with a handsaw. However, I find this method to be slow and less accurate than whittling the tenon.

A tool specially designed to cut tenons is the fastest, most accurate way of making precise tenons. The cone-shaped cutters come in a variety of sizes and are available from wood-working or craft stores. They attach to a hand drill or electric motor and cut tenons in a matter of seconds. Once you have used a tenon cutter, it is hard to be humble enough to go back to the handmade technique.

Fitting the Joints

With your tenon and mortise cut, it would seem a simple business to fit the frame together and glue it up. However, it is very difficult to get every tenon or mortise dead straight, especially if you are working with hand tools. Adjustments must be made to get a proper fit, such as rotating the side rail until the best fit is achieved or trimming a tenon so that it will sit properly in the mortise.

When an artisan is fitting together several pieces that make up part of a frame, things can get trickier still. I always build each piece of a frame by introducing one new element at a time. This way you can

Rope is used to hold the joints together so the glue can set up under pressure.

25

identify the joint that is not fitting properly and make adjustments. (It definitely helps to mark the pieces so that they are reassembled in a similar fashion each time.) Only once you are completely satisfied with the fit should the joints be glued. Not all joints need to be glued—some, especially those that are not of structural significance, can be left to float.

To glue the joints, use wood glue, commonly called carpenter's glue. It comes in different formulations for interior and exterior applications. Apply glue to both the tenon and the mortise. Reassemble all the pieces, and make sure that everything still fits together properly. A rubber mallet always comes in handy for convincing the joints to get together.

The glue must be under pressure to set up properly while it is drying. To squeeze the whole structure together, loop rope around the joint and tighten it by twisting a small stick in the rope. You will need at least two ropes for the pressure on the structure to remain equal. Tighten the ropes evenly until the excess glue is squeezed out of the joints; clean up the excess glue with a damp cloth. Leave the ropes on for at least 24 hours while the glue dries.

Screwing Joints Together

I prefer to use wood screws, rather than ropes, to hold the joints together while the glue dries. The screws are inserted into the joint from the outside of the log, through the center of the mortise and into the end of the tenon, to pull the joint together. The screws supply support to the joint, but are primarily used to hold the parts tightly together while the glue dries.

After I make a mortise, I drill through the center of it right through to the outside of the log with a small-diameter bit; this provides a channel for the screw.

From the outside of the log, drill a countersunk hole to allow the head of the screw to sit below the surface of the log, making sure that the countersunk hole is deep enough to accept a plug that will hide the screw and give the joint a seamless appearance.

The plug itself can be made with a small stick of the same kind of wood and the same diameter as the hole. Glue the stick into the hole and then cut off the excess with a handsaw. With peeled wood, the plug can then be sanded, but with barked wood, I trim the end with a knife and touch up the plug with a bit of dark wood stain. Another method I use for large-scale pieces is to make the countersink hole with a forstner bit, which

A forstner bit cuts holes with a flat bottom.

A countersink bit cuts a tapered hole for inserting screws.

Screwing from the outside of the joint pulls tenon and mortise together while the glue dries.

Plugs are glued into the holes to hide the screws.

drills a flat-bottomed hole with no taper, and then use a corresponding plug cutter to make plugs that fit perfectly into the holes.

Mortise and tenon construction is a complex process that exercises the brain as much as the muscles. It takes patience to get the best results, providing the challenge as well as the satisfaction that makes a project truly successful.

Repairing Scrapes and Scratches

Green wood is very susceptible to injury, and it is almost impossible to construct a project without compromising the bark in some way. A stray swing of the hammer can contact the bark and leave an unsightly patch of the underlying wood. Of course, no one will ever notice the mistake in the same way as the person who built it will, but when it is so easy to repair, why not strive for perfection? I learned this technique late one night just before Christmas as I was rushing to complete the last of Santa's orders. While moving a just-completed chair to the oiling room, I dropped it down a flight of stairs. In a state of utter despair and with nothing to lose, I decided to camouflage the offending scrapes with some wood stain. I was amazed at how effectively this technique hid the damage.

Apply a dark wood stain liberally to the injury and surrounding area with a cotton swab, let it soak in for a minute, and then wipe off the excess stain with a damp cloth. The stain soaks into the exposed wood fibers and is easily removed from the surface of the bark with a damp rag. Once the piece is oiled, the scrape will disappear as if by magic.

Finishing and Protecting

As with any piece of wood furniture that will be exposed to the elements, some care must be taken to protect a rustic furnishing. The main enemy of preservation is the sun; its ultraviolet rays will break down the wood and open the surface to water and insects. Fortunately, there are many ways to protect wood from UV radiation.

A variety of natural and synthetic finishes can be applied, including oils, varnishes, and waxes. Any of these finishes will prolong the life of your furniture, but my philosophy is that the curing process of the wood is as important as the finish that is applied. I like to have the piece of furniture dry indoors without

exposure to the sun. Letting the wood dry prior to construction is the best method of achieving this, but obviously, this is not possible with bent furniture.

Linseed oil should be applied to green wood shortly after construction and the wood left to dry where its exposure to the sun is limited. The oil will allow the wood to dry more slowly. If you can't store a piece inside while it dries, find a shady spot in the garden for its first phase of life—trees are still one of the most effective UV-blocking agents out there.

If you choose to use linseed oil, follow these simple steps. Mix double-boiled linseed oil in equal amounts with a solvent such as Varsol, paint thinner, etc. Brush the mixture on all surfaces and allow the piece to sit in a shaded, well-ventilated area. It should be dry enough to use in 24 hours. A chair will require about 1 cup

Graphite can be used to camouflage the fresh cuts on the barn board slats.

(250 mL) of the mixture. One coat is sufficient, but a second coat the next day will add an extra layer of protection.

It is best to clean and oil your furniture every spring to remove winter dust and to protect it from summer moisture. Indoor furniture should be good for at least three years before re-oiling is necessary. Oiling brightens the colors of the wood and leaves a glossy finish, so you may want to oil more often for aesthetic reasons.

Another important preservation technique is to remove outdoor furniture from exposure to winter weather. Storing your furniture in a garden shed or even a sheltered spot under a tarp will add years to its life.

27

For garden structures and furniture that are constantly exposed to the sun and weather, a more rigorous protocol is required. Once the piece is completely dry, apply an exterior varnish that contains an UV-blocking agent. There are a myriad of products available at the local paint supply store; simply ask a knowledgeable clerk to recommend a product and be careful to apply it under the appropriate climatic conditions so that the finish will set up properly. I use a spar varnish (boat varnish, to the land lover) that requires hot, dry weather and exposure to UV radiation for the blocking agent to be activated.

Even with the best finishes, Mother Nature will work relentlessly to reclaim her wood, so maintain a diligent watch and renew the finish when required. Surfaces that directly face the sun require the most protection and will need touch ups more often than other surfaces.

Safety in the Workshop

Working safely is paramount to being a true artisan. A carpenter friend told me he knew he had achieved a high level of craftsmanship when he couldn't remember the last time he had smacked a finger with his hammer.

Safety largely comes down to common sense. A clean work area and a healthy amount of respect for the tools you use will go a long way toward preventing an accident. Make sure that your eyes and ears are always protected, especially when using power tools.

Fatigue and inattention are probably the two biggest contributing factors to accidents in the workshop. Never work when you are exhausted, and try to keep distractions to a minimum. Breaks in concentration always result in mistakes. I relish the opportunity to work after hours or on a holiday. I can accomplish far more when I am left to work alone, without interruption.

Attitude

Much has been made of the type of personality that is required to be an underwoodsman. The popular mythology of rustic furniture dictates that all who take up the hobby of working with natural materials must be a little strange, or that a long beard and a liking for solitude are prerequisites for discovering the secrets of the forest.

Although this mythology may promote the uniqueness of rustic furniture and might even excuse some neglected facial hairs and poor oral hygiene, it is hardly a necessity for learning and enjoying the art of building rustic projects.

Probably the most important skill needed to succeed at any hobby is to adopt an artisan's state of mind. Approach projects as learning experiences, not as something that must be mastered. Even in building a project you have built many times before, you may learn something new.

Take a bit of advice from my grade six teacher who told me to work through a task as though you were explaining it to somebody. Teaching someone else how to do something can be the best way to learn, because if you can't explain what you are doing, then you probably don't really have a firm grasp of what's going on.

Patience is as important as possessing the insight to realize when something is not working. Often the best method of solving a problem involves walking away from the workbench and giving a project the time it needs to evolve. Sometimes a certain piece of wood isn't meant to be mated with a given design, so know when to discard it and try another.

Don't rush projects. Set goals, not deadlines, as deadlines create pressure that is counterproductive to the enjoyment of the creative process. Build for the joy of the labor, not the finished project, and the pleasure and satisfaction of completing a job will find their way to your workbench.

Armchair

The bent willow chair is the most recognizable example of rustic furniture. Everybody knows somebody who has built a rustic chair. There are as many variations on the style of chair as there are types of willow. My design is basic, straightforward, and easily adapted. I always encourage beginners to start with a chair. In building a chair, you will learn all the basic skills required to be a rustic carpenter and it is a highly satisfying experience. The relationship between a chair and its builder is special, because every time you sit on it, some of the satisfaction of building the chair returns.

This chair design is the basis for all frames made in a simple, overlapping rustic style. Once the basics of building a solid frame are mastered, they can be adapted to any project big or small.

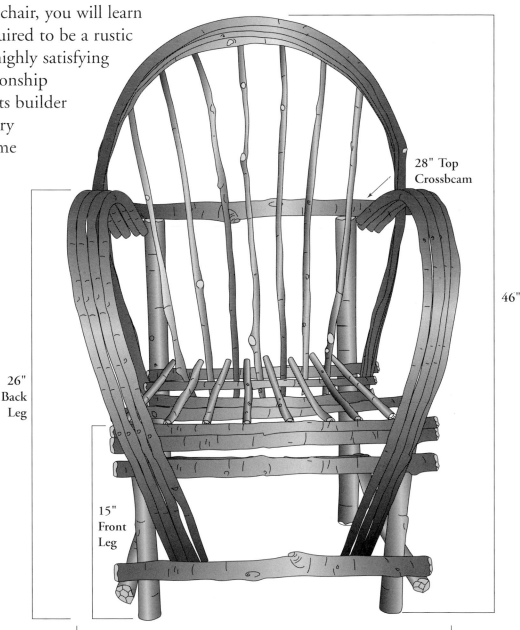

28" Top Crossbeam

46"

26" Back Leg

15" Front Leg

22"

PROJECT REQUIREMENTS

2 front legs—
15" long, 2" diameter

2 rear legs—
26" long, 2" diameter

2 top side rails—
22" long, 1½" diameter

2 bottom side rails—
20" long, 1½" diameter

3 front crossbeams—
22" long, 1½" diameter

3 back crossbeams—
20" long, 1½" diameter

2 diagonal braces—
1½" diameter, length cut to size
(approx. 23")

1 top back crossbeam—
28" long, 2" diameter

8 willow arm benders—
4' long, ¼" diameter

4 willow back benders—
8' long, ¼" diameter

1 buffer strip—
¾" diameter, length cut to size
(approx. 22")

2 seat supports—
1½" diameter, length cut to size
(approx. 22")

9 seat slats—
¾" diameter, length cut to size
(approx. 23")

8 back pieces—
¾" diameter, length cut to size
(approx. 30")

I Building the First Side

Each side consists of: one 15" long, 2" diameter front leg; one 26" long, 2" diameter rear leg; and two side rails, one measuring 22" long, 1½" diameter, the other measuring 20" long, 1½" diameter. Place the legs on a table so that the thicker ends are flush with one side of the table. The side of the table represents the floor that the chair will eventually stand on.

Position the 20" long side rail parallel with the edge of the table, 2½" from the bottom of each leg, with a 1½" overlap on each end. Nail to the legs.

Nail the 22" long side rail to the two legs near the top of the front leg. Determine the exact placement of the top side rail by lining up the intersecting front crossbeam at the joint. Angle the top side rail down toward the back of the chair at a 15-degree slope and nail it into the back leg.

Because the top side rail is longer than the bottom side rail, the back leg will end up sitting at an angle to the front leg. This angle should also be about 15 degrees. The combination of this angle and the angle of the top side rail makes both the seat and the back of the chair more comfortable to sit in.

2 Building the Second Side

Take the first side and flip it over so that the side rails are on your work table. Build the second side directly on top of the first, lining up the side rails with the rails on the first side. Use the hammer handle to straighten and align where needed. Nail in the front two joints, then add the back leg and line up the rear joints. Make sure the bottoms of the legs are flush with the side of the table, and that all angles are equal. You should now have two opposite but matching sides.

3 Connecting the Sides

Connect the sides with crossbeams with a 1½"diameter: 22" long crossbeams in the front and 20" crossbeams across the back. To begin, stand up the two sides and place the front top crossbeam onto the overlap of the top side rails and nail it into the legs.

You want good contact between the crossbeams and the side rails as this will distribute the weight the chair will bear. Therefore, angle the nail slightly downward so you are forcing the crossbeam down onto the overlap as well as holding it against the leg (see photo 3.1). The angle of the nail should be no more than 10 degrees.

Alternate attaching front and back crossbeams to help keep the chair frame square. Once you have three of the six crossbeams attached, start checking that the frame is square. Stand back from the frame and make sure that the legs are aligned with each other. The frame is still quite adjustable at this point, making corrections easy (see photo 3.2). Add the remaining three crossbeams, checking throughout that the chair remains relatively square and that the tops of the back legs are aligned.

4 Adding the Side Brace

The side brace is placed on the side of the frame, fitted in front of the overlap at the bottom back crossbeam. It angles up to fit behind the overlap of the middle front crossbeam and the front leg. Mark and cut the brace so it fits tightly, allowing no movement of the frame, and then nail the brace into the legs. This brace steadies the chair front to back.

5 Nailing the Overlaps

Now that the frame is steadied front to back, nail all the overlaps at the joints. This will solidify the frame and prevent side-to-side swaying. Since these nails go into the ends of the logs, they may have a tendency to split the wood. To avoid this, try flattening the tips of the nails by tapping the point a few times with a hammer. With a dulled tip, the nail is less likely to find its way between the wood fibers and cause a split.

6 Attaching the Top Crossbeam

The top crossbeam measures 28" long, 2" diameter. Make sure that this piece has a straight edge along the back of the seat. The seat slats will rest against this crossbeam, so the comfort of the back requires a flat surface. Center it on top of the back legs and double nail into the legs. Again, nail points should be dulled to prevent splitting the legs. Once the top crossbeam is in place, your frame is finished. It should be solid and allow no movement. If it is unstable, nail any loose joints again.

7 Pre-bending Willows for the Arms

Each arm is made up of four willow benders, bent and nailed one at a time onto the frame. You will need eight benders, each 48" long, ¾" diameter at the thick end. Bend the willow across your knee, working from the thick end to the thin end and making a fulcrum point every 5" or so. The willow should be gently shaped into a curve. (See "Bending Wood" in Chapter Four for more details on pre-bending willow.)

8 Positioning the Arms

Placement of the first bender is vital, because it will determine the shape of the arm and because it must be positioned to leave room for three more benders to be added. I use my index finger as a measure, placing the thin bender end one finger length (approximately 3") inside the front leg and one finger length from the end of the top front crossbeam (see photo 8.1). This allows room for more benders and makes the benders flare out consistently.

Position the thin end of the bender behind the bottom front crossbeam and in front of the top front crossbeam. Bend the willow in an arch, then nail the thick end into the side of the back leg, with the bender resting against the underside of the top front crossbeam (see photo 8.2). Tack the bender into the top front crossbeam, leaving the nail head up so it can be removed easily.

With one bender tacked into position on each side, adjustments can be made to level the two arms. Measure the distance from the floor to the high point in the arch of the arm piece. Raise or lower the other side to match this measurement. Nail the thin end of the bender into both the top front crossbeam and the bottom front crossbeam.

33

9 Adding More Benders

Add the remaining benders one at a time, alternating sides so the stresses on the frame remain equal. The second bender is fitted beside the first bender. Cut the thick end of the second bender and nail it to the top front crossbeam, fitting it tightly against the previous one. Work toward the thin end (at the bottom), nailing the benders together in three or four spots.

Pre-drill holes for the nails, being careful not to drill more than ¼" deep. These pre-drilled channels aim the nails into the anchor bender. The nails must bite firmly into the two benders to hold them together while they dry. Pick your nailing spots carefully, making sure that the benders fit well together. Do not attempt to force gaps together, as they will tend to separate over time and show the nails. If two benders will not sit well together, try double nailing them from opposing angles.

34

10 Bending the Back

Pre-bend four 96" long, 1" diameter willow pieces before fitting them on the frame. Using the best piece first, nail the thick end onto the inside of the top side rail (see photo 10.1). Bend it around the outside of the arms and then fasten it loosely to the inside of the other top side rail. Once you set the curve to the height you want, nail the end into the side rails and the top crossbeam on both sides. Nail three additional benders to the frame and to each other. Alternate the side from which you start each bender to help balance the curve (see photo 10.2).

11 Installing the Seat

The seat is composed of nine 24" long, ¾" diameter pieces for seat slats, and one 22" long, ¾" diameter piece that fits across the front of the seat to act as a buffer strip for the backs of your legs. The seat also requires two supports, which are nailed across the top of the two top side rails. These supports are ¾" diameter, and cut to length to fit onto the side rails.

One support is placed slightly forward of the middle of the seat (see photo 11.1), while the other fits up against the back legs. Because this rear support will also anchor the vertical back pieces, it must be straight in order to create a comfortable back in the chair. Both seat supports are nailed into the top side rails.

Position the ¾" diameter buffer strip along the top front crossbeam (see photo 11.2). It should fit in front of the apex of the log, allowing room for the slats to be nailed into the crossbeam. This strip receives a lot of traffic, so attach it securely with five nails.

Next, cut your seat slats to size and whittle the ends. Nail in the front ends only (see photo 11.3). Use dry willow to fill in the seat, as it will not shrink, crack, or leave your nails standing high. If you use green willow, drill the holes in the seat slats larger than the diameter of the nail shaft to allow for shrinkage. The nail head should be large enough to hold the slat in place.

12 Filling in the Back

The eight back pieces are also ¾" diameter, with the length cut to size. One fits in between each seat slat. Cut the pieces to approximate length and whittle the ends. Again, use dry wood for this application. Nail the thick ends into the rear seat support below the level of the seat slats. The tops are then double nailed into the back of the curved benders. Cut off the excess length after the back supports are firmly attached.

13 Securing the Seat Slats

Pre-drill holes and nail the back of the seat slats into the crossbeam in the back of the seat.

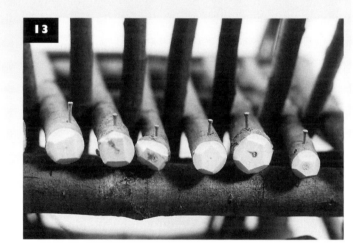

14 Relax in New Chair

A long, cool beverage would make an excellent companion.

Log Vase

This log vase was inspired by a customer who confessed it was not at all what she had in mind when she dictated her idea to me a week or so before, but she liked it and she took it anyway. Its lofty elegance appears simple to create, but as you are about to find out, it requires a fair bit of work. I have found that the smaller the project, the harder it is to build; small items are less forgiving and demand patience and accuracy.

Depending on the size you want, this plan can be adapted to function as several different pieces—a vase, a planter, or even an umbrella stand. It is the same basic design as most baskets and requires the same skills to build.

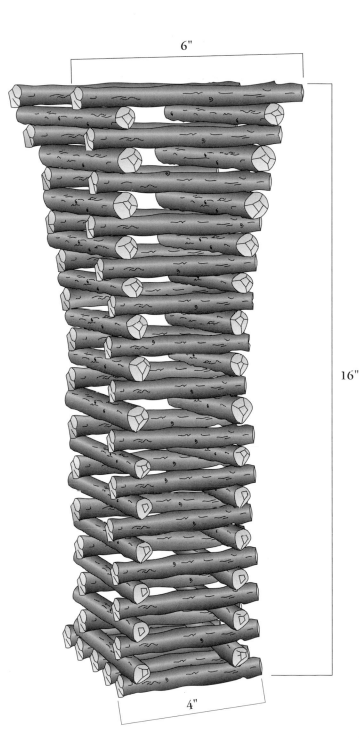

PROJECT REQUIREMENTS

20 to 30 logs for base and bottom—
4" long, ½–¾" diameter

20 to 30 logs for upper part—
½–¾" diameter, length cut to size (maximum 8")

1 Preparing the Wood

Cut at least twenty 4" pieces of ½" to ¾" diameter willow. Whittle the ends into a slightly rounded shape.

2 Building the Base

Choose four straight pieces and join them at the corners with a finishing nail. Pre-drill the nail holes with a small drill bit. Pre-drilling helps you aim your nail more accurately, while also allowing some room for the log to shrink around the nail. The channel created by the bit should be about two-thirds the length of the nail, allowing the last one-third of the nail to bite into the log.

Fill in the space between the two end logs with pieces placed tightly together (see photo in step 4). Once all the pieces are in place, check to make sure they are relatively level and then double nail each joint.

3 Adding Layers

Start adding layers to the filled-in side of your base by choosing two similar logs out of the pile. Nail the logs on two at a time, making sure they are level. Double nail the joints and add the next layer. Add layers until you have ten layers above the base.

4 Increasing the Log Length

Once you have ten layers added to the base, add new logs, increasing their length by 1" each layer. The vase will start to flare outward, and you will have to increase the length of your logs proportionally until you are happy with the vase height.

When making this project as a planter or an umbrella stand, multiply all measurements by at least three. The planter stand will need a shelf built to fit in at a point about two-thirds of the total planter height. This shelf can be built using the same techniques used for filling in the base, that is, by filling in the space between the end logs at the level you want the shelf to sit.

39

Cedar-top Dining Table

This surprisingly simple project proves useful on a daily basis. An employee of mine once asked, "What is the use of feeding a man if he doesn't have the dignity of a table and chair where he can enjoy his meal?" Obviously this person was thinking outside the box in terms of global issues. His calling was beyond my humble ambitions, but his point was well taken.

The top in this project requires some know-how and a router to make the tongue-and-groove edges on the boards, or it can also be made simply with a plank or a slab top—there are many options when it comes to tabletops. The types of wood that are available are as varied as the trees in the forest, and when you start to introduce other elements like stone, glass, or ceramics, the possibilities are endless.

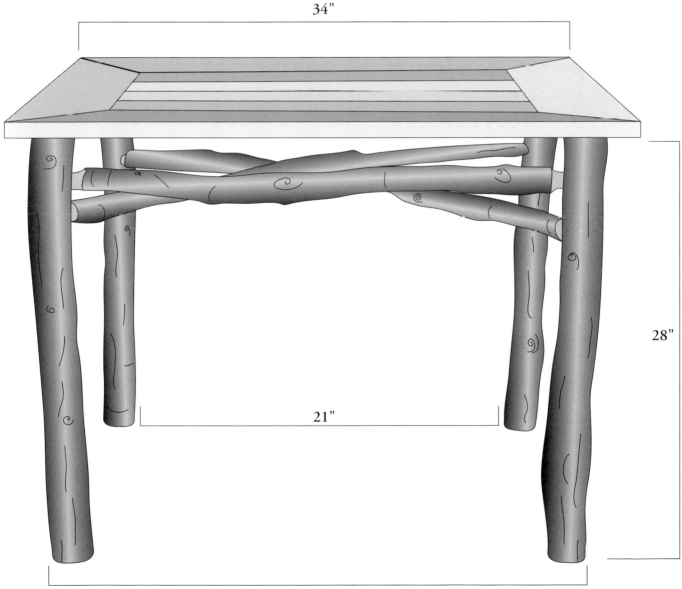

PROJECT REQUIREMENTS

9 cedar boards for top—
34" long, 6" wide, 1" thick

2 braces for table top—
32" long, 1½" square

4 table legs—
28" long, 2" diameter

2 side rails—
1½" diameter, length cut to size
(approx. 22")

2 crossbeams—
1½" diameter, length cut to size
(approx. 22")

2 diagonal braces—
1½" diameter, length cut to size
(approx. 28")

1 A Fitted Tabletop

For this particular project, we are making a tabletop using eight cedar planks: four middle pieces and four edge pieces. The middle slats have a ¼" centered tongue that fits into a centered groove in the four edge pieces. The edge pieces fit together with 45-degree corners.

The edge pieces must be cut and fitted before the length of the middle slats can be determined. The top in this project is 34" square, that is, the outside measurement is 34" on all four sides. Using 5½" wide boards, cut the middle slats to approximately 23½" in length, including the tongue. This may be an area of adjustment that requires a good deal of patience.

Adjust the router to cut a ¼" groove in the middle of the inside edge (the shorter side) of each outside piece. Cut centered tongues, ¼" in thickness, on both ends of each of the four middle slats and fit the whole lot together making adjustments where necessary. Countersink one screw into the outside of each corner so that the 45-degree corners tighten and pull the whole structure together.

2 Reinforcing the Tabletop

Use braces made out of pieces of 1" by 6" plank to reinforce the corners on the underside of the tabletop. Countersink and pre-drill holes into the top to prevent the wood from splitting. Place at least four wood screws in each corner—two for each plank.

3 Bracing the Tabletop

After the corners have been reinforced, the inside slats should have supports installed across their width and connected to the edge pieces. These braces should be 1½" square and approximately 32" long. Screw them in under the tabletop, both into the edge pieces and the inside slats, at least 20" apart.

43

4 Building the Base

The table base employs mortise and tenon construction. Each side consists of two legs 28" long, 2" diameter that are connected by a crossbeam inserted 3" from the top of the legs. The crossbeams will run parallel to the support braces installed under the tabletop. Line up two of the legs with the corner support braces, then measure and cut the crossbeams to fit (see photo 4.1). In this case, the total width of each end worked out to be 23".

Drill a countersunk hole into each mortise from the outside of the leg so that a wood screw can be inserted to pull the tenon tightly into the mortise. Check that everything fits, then disassemble the joints, glue all the pieces, and reassemble the parts. Insert the wood

screw into the drilled hole, tightening the joint until glue squeezes out (see photo 4.2). Clean up the glue with a damp cloth.

Repeat this procedure to make the other end.

5 Connecting the Sides

The two ends are connected with tenon crossbeams that fit in 1" from the top of the leg. The top of the legs should fit tightly against the corner support brackets.

Insert an X-brace about 15" from the bottom of each leg to give the structure stability. For the first brace, drill mortise holes, at 45 degrees to each other, 15" up the leg. Cut the tenons to the correct size and length, then fit them into the frame. For the second brace, drill holes and fit the brace 1½" below the first X-brace.

Once you have all the elements fitted, glue the remaining joints. Pre-drill holes through the legs into the brace pieces, and insert wood screws to pull the braces firmly into the joint.

6 Connecting Base and Tabletop

The tabletop should fit nicely onto the top of the base, with the legs sitting snugly against the corner support brackets. The two top crossbeams should be in contact with the two support braces that run under the tabletop. Pre-drill four holes and screw the crossbeams into the braces at each corner of the tabletop.

Now that the table is done, it's time to get started on some chairs.

U-Chair

This extremely comfortable dining-room chair is a simple and easy project that comes together very quickly. The construction is straightforward because the frame is square, with all the joints connected at 90-degree angles. The frame is a little unusual in that the legs are on the outside of the frame and the side rails and overlaps are inside the legs. This reversal enables the arms and back of the chair to be made out of one bent piece of willow, while it also allows for a simple slat seat with clean lines. It can be completed in just a few hours, making an excellent first project.

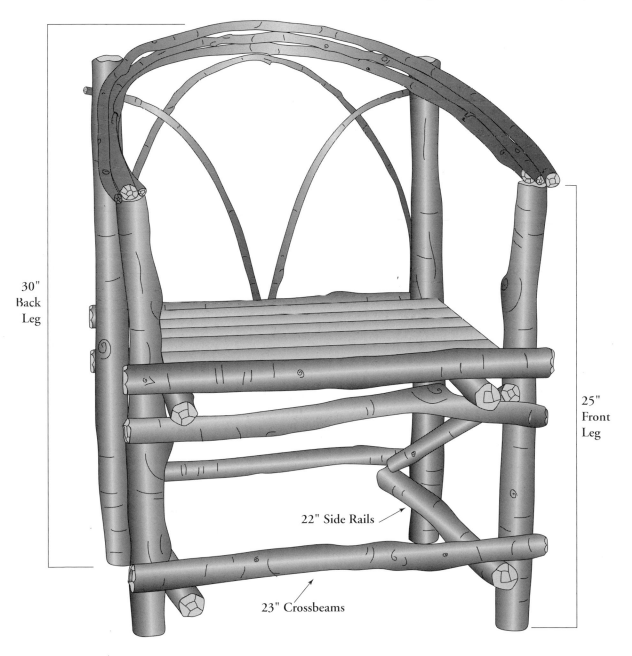

30"
Back
Leg

25"
Front
Leg

22" Side Rails

23" Crossbeams

PROJECT REQUIREMENTS

2 front legs—
25" long, 2" diameter

2 rear legs—
30" long, 2" diameter

4 side rails—
22" long, 1½" diameter

6 crossbeams—
23" long, 1½" diameter

2 diagonal braces—
1½" diameter, length cut to size
(approx. 25")

3 arm and back benders—
4' long, ¾" diameter

7 cedar seat planks—
18½" long, 2¼" wide, 1" thick

3 benders for decoration—
2' long, ½" diameter

1 Building the First Side

Each side consists of: a 25" long, 2" diameter front leg; a 30" long, 2" diameter rear leg; and two 22" long, 1½" diameter side rails. Place the legs on a table perpendicular to the table edge, with the thicker ends flush with one side of the table. The side of the table represents the floor that the chair will eventually stand on.

Connect the side rails to the two legs, starting with the bottom side rail. Position it 2½" from the bottom of each leg, parallel with the edge of the table, with a 1½" overlap on each end. Nail it to the legs.

The top side rail must be a straight, level piece because the seat slats will rest on it. Nail this side rail to the two legs so that its top edge is 15" from the bottom of the legs. It should also be parallel to the edge of the table, with a 1½" overlap on each end.

Stand up the side to make sure that it is square and that the top side rail is level.

2 Building the Second Side

Take the first side and flip it over so that the side rails are on your work table, then build the second side directly on top of the first. Starting with the front leg, line up the side rails with the rails on the first side. Use the hammer handle to straighten everything before nailing. Make sure the bottoms of the legs are flush with the side of the table and that everything is square. Nail in the front two joints, then add the back leg and line up the rear joints. With all four joints complete, you should have two opposite but matching sides.

3 Connecting the Sides

Now that you have two sides, connect them with six crossbeams, each 23" long, 2" diameter. Remember that the side rails should be on the inside of the leg.

Stand the two sides up, with the side rails on the inside. Lay the front top crossbeam onto the overlaps of the top side rails. Now nail it into the legs with the ends of the crossbeam flush with the outside of the front legs.

You want a good connection between the crossbeams and the side rails as this will distribute the weight the chair will bear. Alternate nailing front and back crossbeams to help keep the chair frame square.

Once you have three crossbeams attached to the sides, start checking that the chair frame is square. To do this, stand back from the frame and make sure that the legs are aligned with each other. The frame is still quite adjustable at this point, making corrections easy. Add the remaining three crossbeams, checking that the frame as a whole remains relatively square and that the tops of the back legs are aligned and square.

4 Adding the Side Brace

The side brace is also placed on the inside of the frame. Fit it in front of the overlap at the bottom back crossbeam, and angle it up to fit behind the overlap of the middle front crossbeam and the front leg (see photo 4.1).

This brace can be tricky to measure, so cut it a bit longer than needed and whittle it to size so that it fits snugly behind the middle front crossbeam (see photo 4.2). Nail the brace into the legs. This brace steadies the chair front to back, and so should allow no movement of the frame.

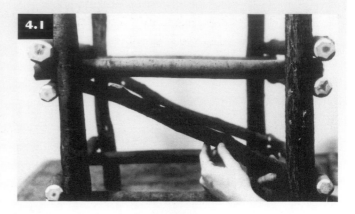

5 Nailing the Overlaps

Now that the frame is steadied front to back, drive nails into all the overlaps at the joints. This will eliminate side-to-side swaying. Since these nails are driven into the ends of the logs, they have a tendency to split the wood. To prevent this, try flattening the head of the nails by tapping the point a few times with the hammer. (See "Dulling the Nail Points" in Chapter Four.)

6 Bending the Arms and Back

Use the same pieces of bent willow to create the arms and back of the chair. Start with 48" long, ¾" diameter benders. You will need at least three pieces. Bend the willow across your knee, working from the thick end to the thin end and making a fulcrum point every 5"

48

or so. The willow should be gently shaped into a U-shaped curve that will fit inside the top of the legs, front and back.

7 Installing the Bent Pieces

First, determine the best way to fit the U-shaped, curved piece of willow inside the four legs. Then, trim the excess off the thick end of the bender. Nail the thick end of the bender into the outside of the top of one front leg (see photo 7.1). Now, fit it inside the back leg on the same side and tack it into position near the top of this leg, leaving room for two more pieces above it (see photo 7.2).

Fit the curve inside the back leg on the opposite side and tack it into the leg at a similar position. The apex of the curve should extend about 6" beyond the two back legs. Bring the thin end of the piece around and nail it into the outside of the top of the other front leg. Trim the excess and whittle the ends. If you are happy with the shape of the curve, double nail the piece into the back legs.

Start the thick end of the second bender on the opposite side from the first bender. Work around the curve, nailing the bender into both the legs and the first bender. This should balance out the curve. Add a third bender, double nailing where possible (see photo 7.3).

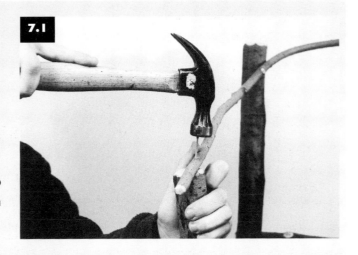

7.1

7.2

7.3

49

8 Installing the Seat

The seat is made up of 1" thick cedar planks that will sit on the two top side rails. In this case, I am using seven planks, each measuring 18½" long by 2¼" wide. Space them evenly and then attach them with a wood screw inserted through the bottom of the side rail (see photo 8.1). Making a pilot hole and countersink channel will help the process go smoothly (see photo 8.2). Access is difficult near the front of the chair because of the position of the diagonal brace, so try drilling at an angle from the outside of the frame. (A stubby screwdriver will also come in handy.)

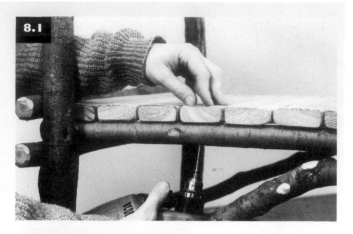

9 Adding Decorative Loops

Three loops of small willow are used to decorate the back of the chair between the top of the seat and the bent willow pieces. The first is an inverted U that fits inside the rear legs. It loops up and is nailed first into the bottom of the backrest pieces and then into the back leg on the opposite side (see photo 9.1).

Two more pieces are nailed into the middle of the top back crossbeam, looping outward, crossing the inverted U, and then nailed into the back of the rear legs (see photo 9.2).

Standing Bird Feeder

This portable bird magnet will attract winged tourists from near and far. Put out the food and your feathered neighbors will follow. It is a great way to relate to nature, no matter where you live or how big your outdoor space is. Be wary of saboteur squirrels or other four-legged bird-watchers.

Provided with a safe feeding spot, birds will flock to your yard. Birds eat a lot, some species up to one-third of their body weight each day, and they are amazing to watch, like little live planes that buzz your landing pad throughout the year. Place the feeder outside your kitchen window and the dishes will almost wash themselves.

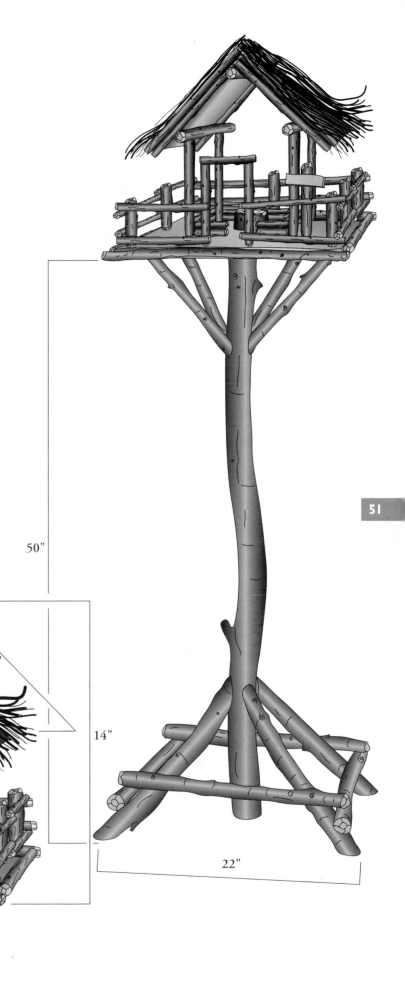

PROJECT REQUIREMENTS

1 plywood platform—
   16" long, 16" wide, ¾" thick

4 house posts—
   9" long, 1" diameter

7 fence posts—
   4" long, ¾" diameter

2 gate posts—
   6" long, ¾" diameter

3 rafters for roof—
   12" long, 1" diameter

2 plywood pieces for roof—
   12" long, 10" wide, ½" thick

willow branches for roof

1 post—
   55" long, 2½" diameter

willow for bracing post—
   a total of 12' in length, 1½" diameter

1 Preparing the Platform

First, lay out the design of the feeding platform. In this case, we used a slab of pine measuring 16" long by 16" wide, and ¾" thick. Drill holes into the slab to set posts for the house and posts for the fence. The position of the house and fence posts are marked on the top of the slab. The house requires four posts, covering an 8" square area in the middle of the platform. The fence requires three holes on two sides, plus one hole in the middle of the back and two holes for the gate posts along the front, for a total of nine holes around the edge of the platform. All holes are drilled ¼" deep into the slab with a ½" paddle bit.

Drill a 1" diameter hole through the center of the slab. This will be used to attach the platform to the stand.

For a bit more fun, add one more hole near the front fence to anchor a signpost that says "No Squirrels Allowed."

2 Installing the Posts

Four posts 9" long, with a ½" tenon, are glued into the four inner holes of the platform. Between these posts, build walls consisting of three horizontal pieces.

Next, seven 4" posts with ½" tenons are glued into the holes around the edges of the platform. The two holes in the front of the platform receive 6" posts to frame the gate-

52

way. All the posts are glued and then nailed from the bottom of the platform to hold them firmly in place while the glue dries.

3 Building the Fence

Add the rails of the fence by nailing them into the fence posts (an air stapler was used on this project).

4 Assembling the Roof

Take two 1" by 10" boards and cut them into 12" pieces. Nail these pieces together along the 10" side at a 90-degree angle. A 12" long rafter is nailed into the underside of the roof (see photo 4.1). The roof is then nailed onto the top of the side rafters. Double nail these joints.

Place two 12" long logs across the top of the center posts to serve as rafters on the outside edges. These should run front to back (see photo 4.2).

53

5 Thatching the Roof

The thatch on the top of the roof is made from the ends of willow branches. First, edge the roof with ¼" diameter sticks. Next, cover the top with branches stapled into the roof (see photo 5.1).

Trim the ends of the thatch, leaving 1" to 2" hanging over the bottom edge of the roof (see photo 5.2).

6 Building the Stand

The post and all the pieces for the base stand should be made out of dry wood so that the joints will not shrink and loosen over time.

For the stand, use a post that measures 55" long, 2½" diameter. Cut a 3" long, 1" diameter tenon on one end of the post. Cut the post 2" below the base of the tenon to form a cap that will hold the platform to the base (see photo 6.1). Trim the tapered part of the tenon to allow the underside of the cap to fit tightly against the top of the platform (see step 8).

Drill four countersunk holes in the top of the cap; it can then be fastened with wood screws through the platform and into the post (see photo 6.2).

Drill a 2¼" deep hole, with a 1" diameter, into the end of the post to accept the cap tenon.

54

7 Building the Base

The bottom of the post is supported by four legs. Cut the legs at an angle of about 35 degrees, then screw and double nail the legs into the post (see photo 7.1).

Connect the four legs with braces that are screwed into the legs. The braces should overlap and be nailed into each other (see photo 7.2). The bottom should be very solid at this point. If there is any play in the base, re-fasten the pieces until they are stable. Trim the legs as needed to make sure that the post stands upright and level.

8 Attaching the Platform

The platform is attached to the base stand using the cap you made in step 6. Place the platform on the base and glue the tenon into the hole on the top of the post (see photo 8.1). Four wood screws can then be used to reinforce the cap and pull all the pieces together (see photo 8.2).

55

9 Bracing the Platform

Four braces are screwed into the post and the underside of the platform, similar to the legs at the base of the post. This should make the platform solid.

10 Dinner's Served!

Add birdseed to the feeder and enjoy the show!

Small Garden Bench

This quaint little bench is perfect for a boot change or a sit down. Either in an entrance or out in the yard, it is a beautiful yet functional little gem. A rack for boots and mitts might be worth considering if it is to be used in a mud room.

18"
Legs

30"

19"

PROJECT REQUIREMENTS

4 legs—
18" long, 2½" diameter

4 side rails—
16" long, 1½" diameter

4 crossbeams—
28" long, 1½" diameter

35 to 40 seat slats—
½–¾" diameter, length cut to size
(approx. 20")

2 willow benders for arms—
15" long, ½" diameter

1 willow bender for decoration—
3' long, ½" diameter

6 to 10 willow branches
(for weaving around arms)

Building the Bench Ends

The frame of this small bench consists of four legs connected at the top and bottom by rails, using a mortise and tenon joint. Start by building the two sides of the bench. Each side will have two legs measuring 18" long, 2½" diameter, and two side rails, measuring 16" long, 1½" diameter. Drill two holes into each leg. The holes should be 1" in diameter, with one hole made 4" from the top of the leg, and the other 2½" from the bottom. Cut a 1" tenon on each end of the side rails, and insert these pieces into the leg holes. The sides of the bench can then be glued and tied (see "Fitting the Joints" in Chapter Four) and left to dry overnight.

An alternate method to hold the joint together while the glue dries is to use a wood screw that is countersunk from the outside of the leg into the tenon. (See "Screwing Joints Together" in Chapter Four).

58

2 Connecting the Ends

Once the ends are finished, drill 1" diameter holes 1½" from the top of the inside of the leg and 4" from the bottom of the leg. The two sides are then connected with crossbeams measuring 28" long, 1½" diameter, with a 1" diameter tenon on each end. It is important to choose a straight, flat piece for the top front and top back crossbeams because the seat slats will be nailed directly to these beams. If a boot shelf is required for the bottom, take care to select suitable bottom crossbeams. Otherwise, the bottom and side rails can allow for a little more artistic license.

3 Installing the Seat

The seat for this bench will consist of slats made from ½" to ¾" diameter sticks, all fastened side by side along the front and back top crossbeams.

Cut slats longer than needed, making sure to use the straightest parts of the sticks. Fashion the seat as level as possible. At the same time, alternate the thick ends of the slats front and back to keep the width of the seat even as you work from one side to the other.

It is important that the slats be well secured to the top rails. They will stabilize the frame and, over time, reduce the bench's tendency to sway. The seat slats should be cross nailed both front and back, and fitted tightly side by side. Use slats that have already dried because they will not shrink in diameter.

Cut the slats to form a curved front edge on the bench by temporarily attaching a dried, curved willow bender to the top of the front legs to act as a guide.

4 Building the Side Handles

Start with a piece of willow 15" long, with a small diameter. Form this piece into an arch on the inside of the legs, and nail into place (see photo 4.1). Weave a branch end from a bender around the original willow, securing the thicker end to the bench leg. Weave another branch end from the opposite side, adding more branches to the weave if necessary (see photo 4.2).

The weave should hold with a little tension, but a discreetly placed piece of garden wire can easily be employed to train any errant branch tips.

5 Custom Finishing

The design possibilities are limitless when it comes to finishing a project. In this case, one simple curved piece was added to the front of the bench.

Square Basket

This simple basket-making technique can be modified or adapted to make a whole range of different projects—simply alter the dimensions and design. These baskets are great for many applications, such as storage, potted plants, or filling with gifts.

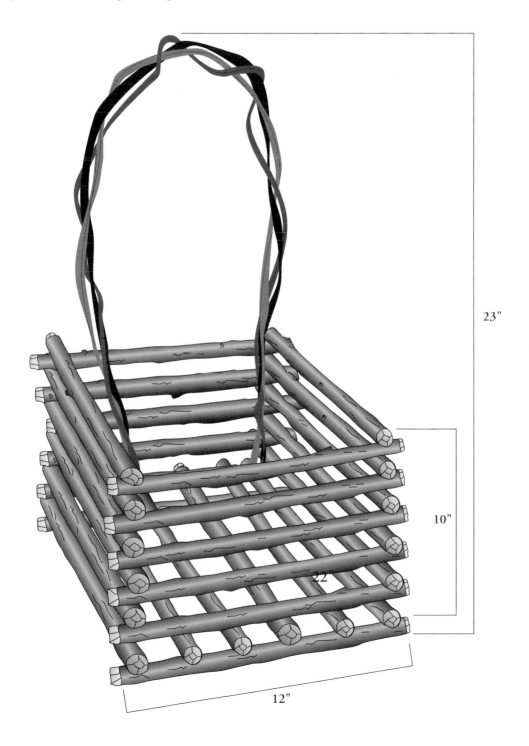

23"

10"

22"

12"

PROJECT REQUIREMENTS

24 willow sticks—
14" long, ¾" diameter

2 willow branches for handle—
30" long, ½" diameter

Plenty of finishing nails

1 Cutting the Sticks

Cut up a good number of ¾" diameter willow pieces into sticks 14" long. Cut more pieces later if you find you don't have enough. Whittle the ends of the willow.

2 Making the Base

The base is made up of four 14" long pieces, nailed together in a square. Pre-drill channels for all the nails and double nail all the pieces. Pre-drilling not only helps to avoid splitting the wood, but also guides the nails right where you want them to go (see photo 2.1).

The base is filled in with more pieces. The bottom can be solid or have gaps, as this project does (see photo 2.2).

3 Building the Sides

Once the base is complete, flip it over and start adding two pieces of equal diameter to each side. Double nail each joint, being careful not to hit the nails in the level below. Build up the sides until the basket is at the desired height. In this basket, nine more levels were added for a total of ten (including the base).

4 Making a Handle

The handle is made from the end of a bender. Use one with a few branches that can be woven to give the handle some volume. For the best results, make each handle using two bender ends; balance the thick and thin ends, and weave the branches together to make the handle fuller and more even (see photo 4.1). Pre-bend the handle pieces to give them a nice, arched shape and then attach them to the inside of the two bottom end pieces (see photo 4.2).

The handle should also be secured to the outside of the top end pieces with nails and garden wire (see photo 4.3).

Loveseat

This project is very similar to the bent willow chair featured earlier in the book. The construction is the same, except that the loveseat is twice as wide as the chair. The loveseat combines nicely with a chair or two, and makes a great spot for courting and sparking.

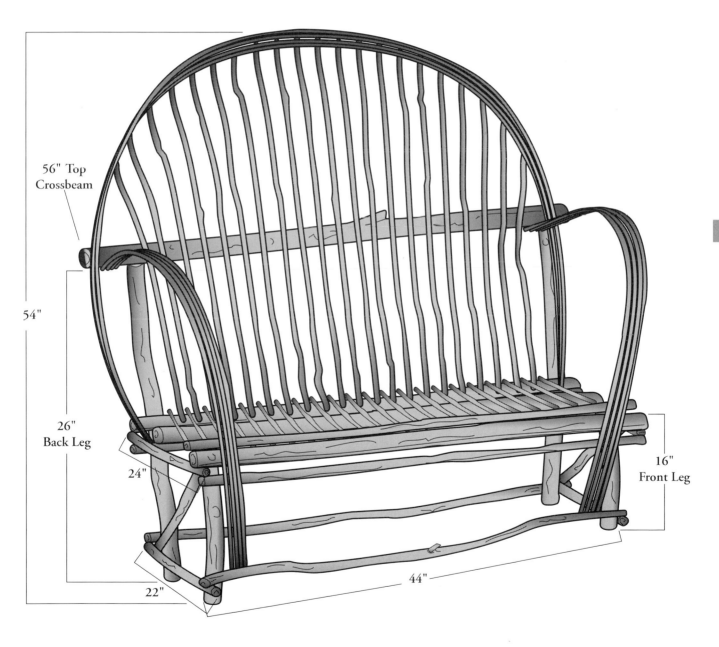

56" Top Crossbeam

54"

26" Back Leg

24"

22"

44"

16" Front Leg

PROJECT REQUIREMENTS

2 front legs—
16" long, 2" diameter

2 rear legs—
26" long, 2" diameter

2 side rails—
22" long, 1½" diameter

2 side rails—
24" long, 1½" diameter

6 crossbeams—
44" long, 1½" diameter

2 side braces—
1" diameter, length cut to size (no more than 30")

1 top crossbeam—
56" long, 2" diameter

8 willow arm benders—
48" long, ¾" diameter

4 willow back benders—
12' long, 1½" diameter

1 buffer strip—
44" long, ¾" diameter

2 seat supports—
44" long, 1" diameter

22 seat slats—
¾" diameter, length cut to size

22 back pieces—
¾" diameter, length cut to size

1 Building the First Side

Each side consists of one 16" long, 2" diameter front leg, one 26" long, 2" diameter rear leg, and two side rails. The rails measure 24" long, 1½" diameter and 22" long, 1½" diameter, respectively. Lay the legs on the table so that the thicker leg ends are flush with one edge of the table. This edge represents the floor that the loveseat will eventually sit on.

Connect the 22" bottom side rail to the two legs and place the side rail parallel with the edge of the table. Position it 2½" up from the bottom of the legs with a 1½" overlap on each end, then nail it to the legs.

Nail the 24" side rail to the two legs near the top of the front leg. Establish the exact position of the top side rail by holding the intersecting front crossbeam at the joint (see photo 1.1), and placing the rail just below the crossbeam. Angle the top side rail down towards the back of the chair at a 15-degree slope and nail it into the back leg.

Because the top side rail is longer than the bottom side rail, the back leg will sit at a 15-degree angle to the front leg (see photo 1.2). These angles make both the seat and the back of the chair more comfortable to sit in.

2 Building the Second Side

Take the first side and flip it over so that the side rails are in contact with the table and begin to build the second side directly on top of the first (see photo 2.1). Start with the front leg, lining up the side rails with the rails on the first side. Use the hammer handle to line up the pieces before nailing (see photo 2.2). Nail in the front two joints, then add the back leg, again lining up the side rails and nail into the back leg. With all four joints nailed you should have two opposite but matching sides.

3 Connecting the Sides

Now that you have two sides, connect them with the 44" crossbeams. Stand up the two sides, placing the top front crossbeam onto the overlap of the top side rails. Nail the beam into the legs. You want good contact between the crossbeams and the side rails to distribute the weight the chair will bear. (A trick that will assure good contact between the overlaps is to angle the nail slightly so that you are forcing the crossbeam down onto the overlap as well as into the leg. The angle of the nail should be no more than 10 degrees.)

Start with the front top crossbeam and alternate adding crossbeams front and back, aiming for a total of six crossbeams: two on the top front, two on the back top, one bottom front, and one bottom back.

Once you have three crossbeams attached, start checking that the frame is square. Stand back and check that the legs are aligned with each other. The frame is still quite adjustable at this point, making correction easy. Add the remaining three crossbeams, checking throughout that the frame remains relatively square and that the tops of the back legs are aligned.

4 Adding Side Braces

The side brace is placed on each side of the frame, fit in front of the overlap at the bottom back crossbeam. It angles up to fit behind the overlap of the middle front crossbeam and the front leg. Mark and cut the brace so that it fits tightly, allowing no movement of the frame, and then nail the brace into the legs. This brace helps steady the chair front to back.

5 Nailing the Overlaps

Now that the frame is steadied front to back, nails are driven into all the overlaps at the joints. This will make the frame solid and prevent side to side swaying. Since these nails are driven into the ends of the logs, they may have a tendency to split the wood. A good trick to prevent this is to flatten the tips of the nails by tapping the point a few times with the hammer.

6 Attaching the Top Crossbeam

The top crossbeam measures 56" long, 2" diameter. Make sure that this piece has a straight edge along the back of the seat. The seat slats will rest against this crossbeam so the comfort of the back requires a flat surface. Lay the crossbeam on top of the back legs and double nail it into the top of the legs. Again, nail points should be dulled to prevent splitting the legs.

With the top crossbeam in place your frame is finished. It should be solid, allowing no movement. If it is not, nail any loose joints again.

7 Pre-bending Willows for the Arms

Each arm is made up of four willows bent and nailed one at a time onto the frame. You will need eight benders, each 48" long, ¾" diameter at the bender's thick end. Bend the willow across your knee working from the thick end to the thin end making a fulcrum point every 5" or so. The willow should thereby be gently shaped into a curve. (See "Bending Wood" in Chapter Four).

8 Positioning the Arms

Placement of the first bender is crucial, because it will determine the shape of the arm; the bender must be positioned so that there is room for the remaining three benders still to be added. Place the thin end of the first bender behind bottom front crossbeam and bend it around the front top crossbeam attaching it to the rear leg under the top crossbeam. Tack the thin end into the top front crossbeam with the nail head

exposed so that it can be easily removed if you have to adjust the bender placement. (Another trick is to use your index finger as a measure, placing the bender's thin end one finger length, or roughly 3", inside the front leg and one finger length from the end of the top front crossbeam. This allows room for more benders and makes the benders flare out evenly.)

With one bender tacked into position on each side, adjustment can be made to level the two arms. Measure the distance from the floor to the high point of the arm piece. Raise or lower the other side to match this measurement. Nail the thin end into both the front top crossbeam and the front bottom crossbeam.

9 Adding More Benders

Begin adding the benders one at a time, alternating sides so that the stresses on the frame remain equal. Once bent, fit the second bender along the existing arm to find the section of new bender that best matches the contours of the attached arm. Cut the thick end of the bender and nail it to the top crossbeam, fitting it tightly against the last bender. With the thick end nailed into the frame, work towards the thin end, nailing the benders together in three or four spots.

Pre-drill nail holes no more than ¼" deep. This pre-drilled channel helps aim the nail into the anchor bender. The nail must bite firmly into the two benders and hold them together while they dry. Do not attempt to force gaps together, as they tend to separate over time and show the nails. If two benders will not sit well together, try double nailing with nails set at opposing angles.

10 Bending the Back

With the arms completed, start bending the back. Pre-bend four pieces 12" long, 1½" diameter before fitting them on the frame. Use the best piece first and nail the thick end onto the inside of the top side rail. Bend around the arms and nail to the inside of the other top side rail. Once you set the curve to the height you want, nail the bender into the top crossbeam on both sides. Nail the three remaining benders to each other and the frame, alternating the side from which you start each time to help balance the curve.

11 Installing the Seat

The seat is composed of approximately twenty-two ¾" diameter pieces and one piece measuring 44" long, ¾" diameter across the front of the seat to act as a buffer strip for the back of your legs when sitting.

The seat also requires two supports. One is placed slightly forward of the middle of the seat, the other fits up against back legs. The rear seat support must also anchor the vertical pieces that make up the back of the seat to ensure it has a straight edge. Both seat supports are nailed into the top side rails (see photo 11.1).

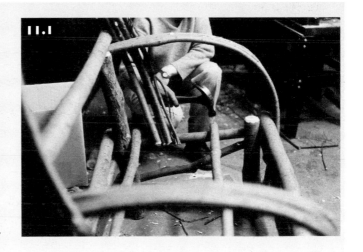

The buffer strip is then positioned along the top front crossbeam (see photo 11.2). It should fit in front of the apex of the log, allowing room for the slats to be nailed into the crossbeam. This strip receives a lot of traffic, so attach it securely with nails every six inches.

Next cut your seat slats to size and whittle the ends, nailing only the front ends. I always use dry willow to fill in the seat because it will not shrink, crack, or leave the nails

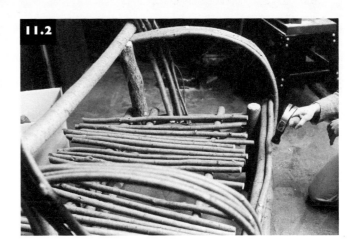

standing high. If you use green willow, drill the holes in the seat slats oversized in relation to the diameter of the nail shaft to allow for shrinkage. The nail should have a head large enough to hold the slat in place.

12 Filling in the Back

The back slats are also ¾" diameter pieces, with the length cut to size. One fits in between each seat slat (see photo 12.1). Cut the slats to approximate length and whittle the ends. Again, use dry wood for this application. Nail the thick ends into the rear seat support below the level of the seat slats. The tops are then double nailed into the back of the curved benders (see photo 12.2). Cut off excess length after back supports are firmly attached.

13 Nailing the Seat Slats

Nail the backs of seat slats into the crossbeam at the back of the seat. This will complete the loveseat.

Side Table

This side table is a quick project that can easily be altered in size or height to suit your needs, and the simple slat top can be made out of any type of wood. The shelf is perfect for books, glasses, or a plant in a corner of your home.

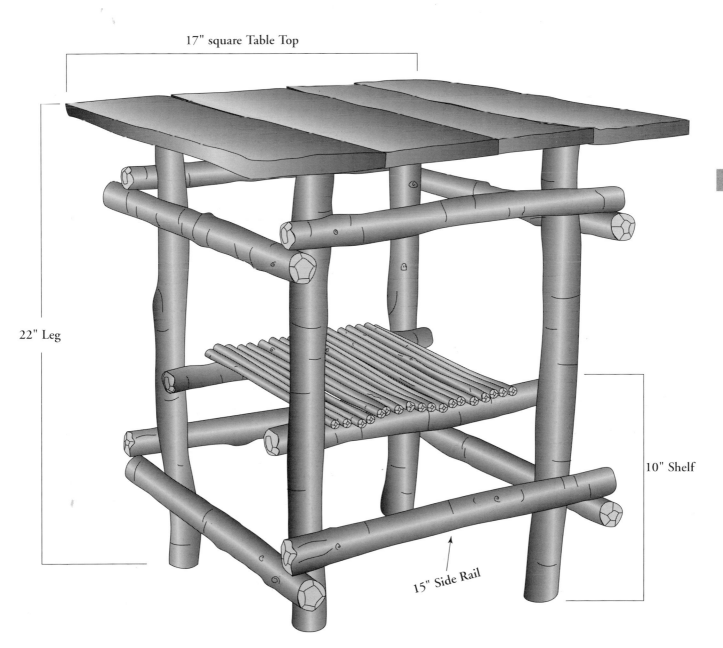

17" square Table Top

22" Leg

10" Shelf

15" Side Rail

PROJECT REQUIREMENTS

4 legs—
22" long, 1½" diameter

4 side rails—
15" long, 1" diameter

4 crossbeams—
15" long, 1" diameter

2 shelf supports—
1" diameter, length cut to size (approx. 13")

15 to 20 shelf slats—
½" diameter, length cut to size (approx. 15")

4 slat boards for top—
17" long, 4¼" wide, 1" thick

2 struts for table top—
15" long, 2" wide, ¾" thick

1 Building the First Side

Each side of the base consists of: two 22" long, 1½" diameter legs, and two 15" long, 1" diameter side rails. Place the legs on the table top with the thick ends flush against one side of the table; this edge represents the floor that the table will eventually sit on. Nail the bottom side rail to the legs 3½" up from the bottom of the leg, with an inch of overlap at each end.

Nail the top side rail into the legs 3½" from the top of each leg with the same 1" overlaps. Stand the side up and make sure it is square. All four legs must be the same length to ensure that the table top will be level.

2 Building the Second Side

Construct the second side by copying the first side. Flip the first side over so that the side rails are lying on the table top, then lay the second set of legs against the legs of the first side. Make sure that the bottoms of the legs are even with each other. Position the side rails on the legs so that they line up with the side rails on the first side. Nail the side rails into the legs as with the first side. You should have two sides that are mirror images of each other.

3 Connecting the Sides

The side are connected by the four remaining crossbeam pieces, each measuring 15" long, with a 1" diameter. These crossbeams are placed on top of the overlapping ends of the side rails and nailed into the legs. Once the crossbeams are nailed into the legs, check to make sure the frame is square and then hammer a second nail into each leg.

4 Nailing the Overlaps

Nail the overlaps of the joints together to stabilize the table. Make sure that a channel is pre-drilled into the overlapping pieces to keep the logs from splitting. (Dulling the heads of the nails will also lower the chances of splitting the log.)

5 Installing the Shelf

Cut two willow logs 13" long, with a 1" diameter to support the shelf. Double nail them to the inside of the legs 10" from the bottom of each leg (see photo 5.1).

Cut pieces 16" long, ½" diameter and place them on the supports so that they overhang by ½" on each end. When you have enough cut to fill the shelf and you are happy with the fit, nail them into the shelf supports (see photo 5.2).

75

6 Making the Tabletop

This table has a simple slat top that is made using barn boards. This project uses four boards 4¼" wide, cut to a length of 17". This will make a 17" square top that will overhang the base by about an inch on each side.

Lay the four slats face down on the table and position the base upside down on the slats. Check to make sure that the base and top are square. The slats are then connected using two struts that cross all four slats.

The struts are made out of pine boards that are 15" long, 2" wide, and ¾" thick. Position the struts so that they touch the inside of the legs. Mark the struts' position on the slats and then remove the base. Mark and drill pilot holes through the pine struts so that each slat is held to the struts with two 1" long wood screws. Insert the screws through the struts into the bottom of the tabletop.

7 Attaching the Top and Base

Place the top on the base and drill a pilot hole through each leg into the strut. Attach the leg to the strut using a wood screw long enough to extend through the leg and at least ½" into the strut. Tighten the screw by hand to reduce the chance that the strut will split.

Coat Rack

This simple, utilitarian project was designed by Mother Nature. It seemed obvious to me that this particular tree, which appeared to have been struck by lightening and had grown around its injury, would make a perfect coat rack. Being open to the design possibilities of oddities presented by the forest is important—often the idea just jumps out at you. These are the kind of projects that make people think underwoodsmen are a little strange.

The base of the coat rack is a slab from an elm tree left on a boulevard by a tree crew. Using a heavy log to construct a base works well in applications in which you want the piece to be sturdy, yet portable. Stumps like this can also be used for bird feeders, signposts, temporary fencing, and so on.

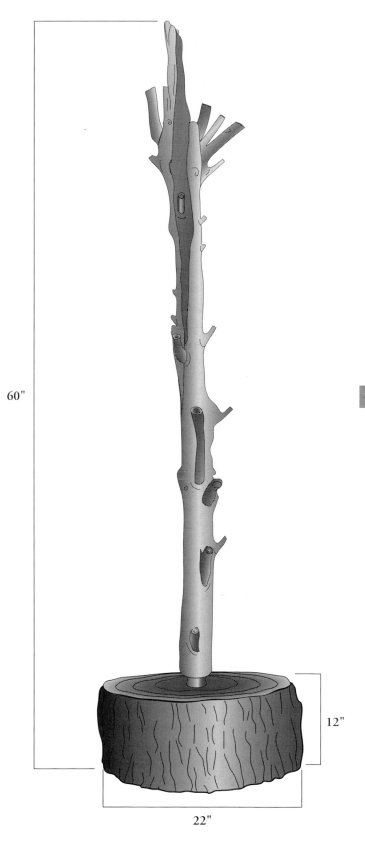

60"

12"

22"

PROJECT REQUIREMENTS

1 log base slab—
  8" to 10" thick, 20" diameter

1 post with lots of branches—
  4' long, 2" diameter

1 Making the Tenon

Allow the willow post to dry, then make a tenon with the largest diameter possible on the bottom.

2 Preparing the Base

Your base log should also be thoroughly dry. When it is dry, drill a large bore hole in the top of the base piece. The mortise should be the same size as the tenon you made in step 1.

3 Gluing the Tenon

Apply wood glue to both surfaces. Place the post into the base, making sure there is a tight fit (see photo 3.1). In this instance the tenon was a little slim, so we added some wood shavings to tighten the fit (see photo 3.2).

4 Screwing Down the Post

On each side of the post, pre-drill a hole through the base slab and into the post, extending each hole through the post and into the base on the opposite side. Fasten the post to the base with a couple of long wood screws to ensure that the post sucks down into the base. The air must be squeezed out of the joint for the glue to set up properly.

5 Finishing

Whittle the ends of the coat hooks, making all surfaces smooth. Give the whole post a light sanding and seal it with a varnish.

Then, as Mother likes to say, "Hang up your coat and stay a while."

Peeled Log Bench

This project is an attractive example of peeled log furniture. Most woods can be peeled, and for this bench we are using peeled laurel leaf willow. The best time to peel wood is when the plant is actively growing. The new layer of wood just under the bark is very moist and will separate easily. Wood peeled at the right time of year is very smooth and requires little sanding. Once the bark has been peeled, the wood will dry very quickly, making it an excellent material for mortise and tenon construction.

46"

36"
Back
Post

28"
Front
Post

17" Seat Height

24" Side Rail

PROJECT REQUIREMENTS

2 front legs—
28" long, 5" diameter

2 rear legs—
36" long, 5" diameter

8 side rails—
2" diameter, length
cut to size (approx. 24")

8 vertical posts for sides—
1" diameter, length
cut to size (approx. 9")

5 crossbeams—
40" long, 2" diameter

7 to 8 vertical back posts—
1½" diameter, length
cut to size (approx. 20")

4 cedar planks for seat—
42" long, 6" wide, 1" thick

1 Drilling Holes for Side Rails

Each side consists of: one 28" long, 5" diameter front leg; one 36" long, 5" diameter rear leg; and four 24" long, 2" diameter side rails. The side rails have a 1½" tenon cut on each end.

Mark the centers of the mortise holes at 6", 14", 16", and 25" from the bottom of each leg. Drill four 1½" wide mortises into each leg about 1½" deep. The side rails that fit into the 14" mortises on each side must be straight, as the seat boards will rest on these logs.

2 Fitting the Side Rails

Start with the top and bottom side rails, plus the two legs. Force the tenons into the mortises using a rubber mallet. The total width of the side should be about 30" once these four pieces are fit together.

Make sure the side is square and the legs sit flat on the floor. Because none of the elements will be perfectly straight, it helps to rotate the side rails in the mortise to determine the best fit.

Once you are happy with the fit, introduce the third and fourth side rails one at a time. Trim the ends of these rails until all the elements fit together easily.

3 Inserting the Vertical Posts

The four vertical posts fit between the top and third side rails; each post measures about 9" long. Although they are decorative, they also help to stabilize the side front to back.

First, make a ¾" tenon on the bottom of each of the four posts. Measure where each post will fit into the third rail, and mark these spots by drilling pilot holes. Remove the third side rail from the legs, and drill the four mortises 1" deep into it, to accept the tenons on the posts (see photo 3.1).

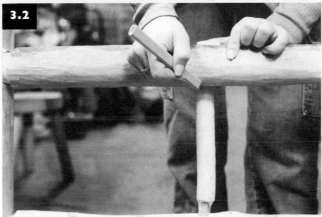

Replace the third side rail into the legs. With the side fitted together, insert the posts one at a time into the third rail. Level each post to determine the spot to drill pilot holes in the underside of the top side rail (see photo 3.2). Remove the top side rail and drill four ¾" mortises into the rail to a depth of 1".

Seat the vertical posts in the mortises in the third side rail and determine the exact length of each post. Insert the posts one at a time, making adjustments where necessary (see photo 3.3).

The whole side should fit back together easily. If it is stubborn, you probably need to trim the vertical posts. The four vertical posts are not fastened into place but float between the side rails.

Repeat steps 1 to 3 to build the other side of the bench.

4 Glue and Screw

Once all the elements of the sides are fitted together, you then drill holes through the outside of the legs that will match up with the tenons. To locate the proper spot for the hole, drill a wood screw from the center of the mortise through to the outside of the leg. (See "Screwing Joints Together" in Chapter Four.)

Once you've located the spots for your holes, drill a countersunk hole from the outside of the log. In this case, we are using a forester bit to drill a ½" hole that will hide the screw head. This hole is filled with a plug later.

Pull the side apart and apply glue to both surfaces of each joint. Gently fit the side back together and insert the screws. The tightening screws should squeeze the excess glue from the joints. Use a damp rag to remove any visible glue.

5 Drilling Holes for the Crossbeams

Drill holes into the inward side of each of the two bench sides—three holes in the rear legs and two in the front legs. The centers of the rear-leg mortises are at 8", 13", and 33" from the bottom. The centers of the front-leg mortises are at 8" and 15" from the bottom. Each mortise should be cut with a 1½" paddle bit to a depth of 1½".

6 Attaching the Crossbeams

The bench requires five crossbeams 40" long, 2" diameter, all with a 1½" tenon cut on both ends. Fit the two sides together with the five crossbeams, adding one piece at a time. Trim the crossbeams to achieve a nice, square fit. Once you have all five crossbeams fitting nicely into the sides, insert vertical posts between the second and third crossbeams in the back of the seat.

7 Inserting the Vertical Posts

Use the same procedure to insert the vertical posts in the back of the seat that you used to fit vertical posts into the sides. Drill mortises for the number of posts that you want along the top edge of the middle-rear crossbeam. Make tenons on both ends of each vertical post. With the bottom of the post seated in each mortise, determine where to locate the mortise in the top crossbeam (see photo 7.1).

Mark the location of each mortise in the underside edge of the top crossbeam and then mark the exact length of each vertical post. Remove the top crossbeam and drill ¾" diameter mortises to a depth of 1" into the underside of the top crossbeam. Fit in the vertical posts one at a time, trimming as necessary (see photo 7.2). These seat posts are not fastened in place.

8 Connecting the Sides

With all the elements of the back fitted into place, the crossbeams connecting the sides can be made permanent with glue and wood screws. Apply glue to the joints when fitting everything back together.

Drill holes to act as channels for the wood screws in each of the crossbeam joints, then countersink the screws so the heads are hidden below the surface of each log. Tighten each joint with wood screws, and clean up any excess glue.

9 Plugging Screw Holes

Use willow dowels to glue plugs in place, and cut off any excess with a handsaw. Sand the plug and wood until they are smooth. A special drill bit is available to make plugs, or see "Screwing Joints Together" in Chapter Four for more details on making plugs.

10 Finishing the Surface

With the frame of the bench complete, give the wood a final sanding and cleaning, and then apply the finish. It's easiest to clean up the edges and ends of the logs as you go, leaving only a final light sanding before the finish is applied. The finish on this project was achieved using a spar varnish with a UV-blocking agent.

11 Installing the Seat

The seat is made up of four 1" by 6" cedar planks that will sit on top of the second side rail. Notch the corners of the planks to fit nicely around the legs (see photo 11.1). Trim the length of the seat planks and fit them into the bench. With all four planks in place, fit a brace across the bottom planks to support the seat (see photo 11.2). The ends of the planks are then attached to the second side rail with screws inserted into pre-drilled channels from underneath the seat (see photo 11.3). The cedar planks need not be protected from the elements, and will be allowed to turn gray slowly over time.

11.1

11.2

11.3

87

Bent Willow Arbor

This is a really fun project that can be built in a variety of sizes, and it will fit just about any part of your garden. An arbor is often directly connected to flora, as well as the odd fauna, and can give your yard height, provide support for your plants, frame an entryway, or just offer a spot to linger.

Planning is crucial before starting any project. Measure the site where your arbor will be placed. Remember that the size and scope of the project are always dictated by the environment in which it will be situated.

In this particular project, we are working with an existing frost fence and gate, along with an air-conditioning unit that interrupts one side of the arbor. Keeping these concerns in mind, we will build a curved-top arbor, that is 10' long, 4' wide, and 7' high, using a simple horizontal cross beam-fill pattern.

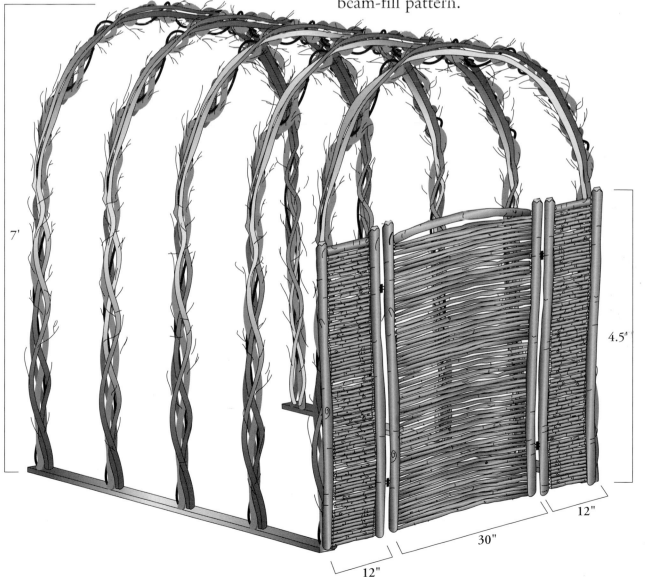

PROJECT REQUIREMENTS

2 anchor beams—
10' long, 4" wide, 6" thick

6 pieces of reinforcement bar—
30" long, ⅜" diameter

14 willow benders for arches—
10' long, 1½" diameter

10 to 15 willow stalks for horizontal beams and fill—
11' long, 2" diameter

1 Preparing the Ground

We will anchor the arbor into two 4" by 6" pressure-treated beams. These beams will then be stabilized using sections of ½" diameter concrete reinforcement bars, each 30" long.

Begin by digging a channel to accommodate each beam. The beams should be placed deep enough that they will not show. When digging the channels, allow some room for leveling and squaring each beam.

2 Preparing the Beams

This project calls for seven arches, spaced 14" apart. Measure and mark your beams, then drill seven holes 2" deep into the beam, using a ½" paddle bit. Three holes for the reinforcement bar should also be drilled along the length of each beam. Because the bar will penetrate the ground up to 24", make sure there is nothing in its path. The length of the bar can be altered if necessary to accommodate ground conditions.

3 Setting the Beams

Once the beams are leveled and squared with each other and their surroundings, hammer the reinforcement bar through the beams to secure their position.

91

4 Pre-bending the Willow

The willow pieces that will be used to make the arches should be bent before they are attached to the beams. Choose two willows of comparable size and thickness and bend them along their length, limbering them up into an arch that will easily fall in between the beams. I've found that fresh wood bends the best, and you can use your knee or foot to shape the willow into an arch about every 6 to 8 inches.

5 Connecting Willow and Beams

5.1

Once all the arch pieces are sorted and bent, you can begin fastening them into the base beams. Set your willows two at a time, working from one end of the beam to the other. Cut off the bottom of your willow arches to ensure they begin bending at the proper height. In this arbor, they should start bending about 40" above the ground. Once trimmed, whittle the bottoms of the willows down to ½" cylinders, each about 2½" long, that can be fitted into a hole in the anchoring beams (see photo 5.1).

The cylinder should fit snugly into the hole. Because you are using fresh wood the willow will shrink a little, so both the cylinder and the hole must be liberally coated with outdoor wood glue. Insert the cylinder into the hole and fasten the willow to the beam with an angled screw (see photo 5.2). The screw should be long enough to go all the way through the willow into the beam on the other side of the hole. Pre-drill the screw path to be sure the screw goes where you want it to go, as well as to minimize the chance of splitting the willow.

5.2

6 Weaving the Arches

Weaving the willow arches is both the most exciting and the most nerve-racking step of the whole process. Weaving may be overstating the process a little—winding is perhaps a better word to describe the technique.

The two main stems are wound around each other with the branches woven in along the way. Don't weave too tightly—leave yourself room for adjustment. Pre-bending the arches will make the process far easier. At this juncture, you will probably need a ladder, as well as another set of hands.

Once you've made a couple of weaves, you can pull the ends down to set the height of the arch. With the height set, continue to weave the branches back down around each other.

Leaving all the branches on these pieces gives you an abundance of material to weave. Dead branches are not much use for weaving but do add volume to the arch. Live branches will weave and hold in place nicely.

The weave should hold together on its own, but for added stability, a small piece of garden wire wrapped around the woven branches will prevent the weave from untangling.

Patience pays at this point, because snapping the willow will damage the integrity of the arch and could mean you have to replace one of the arch pieces.

7 Filling the Frame

Start connecting the arches with horizontal struts (see photo 7.1). Fasten the arches to the struts with nails hammered in at opposing angles for the best hold (see photo 7.2).

The pieces you choose for the horizontal struts should be fairly straight, as your alignment of arches is involved. Once you have a basic framework, you can fill in the space with an endless choice of design possibilities. Often the function plays a crucial role in design decisions.

7.1

7.2

94

8 Protecting the Structure

Protecting the structure is an essential element in the building process. Shortly after finishing the structure, apply a coat of double-boiled linseed oil and a solvent, mixed at a ratio of 1:1. Linseed oil is made from flax seeds and will break down naturally over time, so while it provides protection it will also allow the wood to breathe and dry.

Because we are using fresh wood in this project, we must let the wood dry sufficiently before applying a varnish that will block the sun's harmful ultraviolet radiation. Once the structure has been oiled and is completely dry, apply the spar varnish (boat varnish).

As well, after the oiling is complete, apply a bead of exterior silicone to the bottom of each vertical post to prevent water from seeping into the holes in the base beams. Make sure that the glue you used in each hole has had a chance to dry completely before you apply the silicone sealant.

The base beams can now be covered. Gravel is the best material, but regular soil can also be used. A thin layer of gravel seems to work well, and reduces the chance of rotting. Growing vines over the structure will provide the maximum protection by both shading the wood from the sun and reducing the amount of moisture that reaches it.

Bobsleigh

The many stresses placed on a sleigh demand a solid frame, so I double nail each joint. The entire project is over-designed to ensure that the frame does not become wobbly.

Have the runners made by a metalsmith. I get a 1" piece of wrought iron bent into shape so that it has a running length of 25", that is, 25" on the ground. Three holes are countersunk in each runner so that screws can be driven in from the bottom.

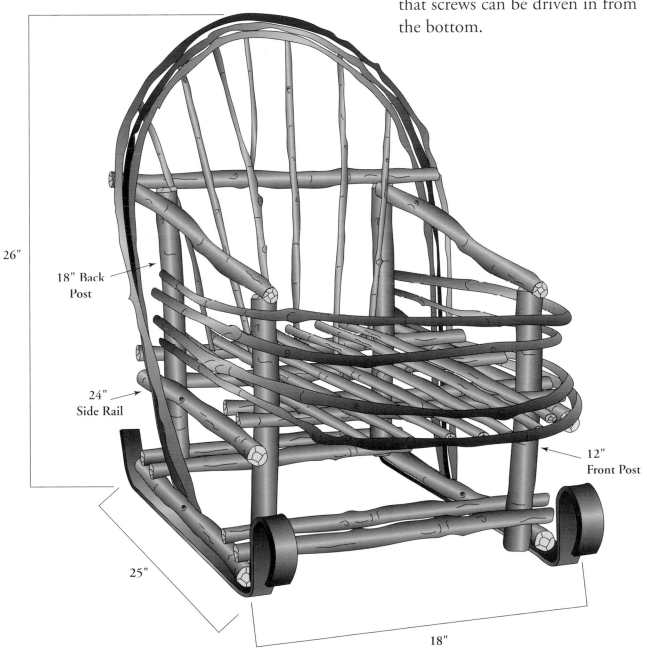

26"

18" Back
Post

24"
Side Rail

12"
Front Post

25"

18"

PROJECT REQUIREMENTS

2 flat iron metal runners—
1" flat iron, bent at both ends, 25" running length

2 front posts—
12" long, 2" diameter

2 back posts—
18" long, 2" diameter

4 side rails—
24" long, 1½" diameter

9 crossbeams—
18" long, 1½" diameter

1 top back crossbeam—
21" long, 1½" diameter

8 willow cockpit and back benders—
4' long, ¾" diameter

2 handle pieces—
1" diameter, length cut to size

15 willow seat and back fillers—
3' long, ¾" diameter

1 pull rope—
10' of ½" rope (optional)

3 jingle bells
(optional)

I Building the Sides

Each side consists of two vertical posts and two side rails. Each front post measures 12" long, 2" diameter; each back post is 18" long, 2" diameter. The two side rails are 24" long, 1½" diameter. The bottom side rail must be very straight to fit along the metal runner. Check that the piece you have chosen will line up with the screw holes on the bottom of the runner.

Nail the side rails to each post. The bottom rail should be flush with the bottom of each post and the top rail nailed onto each post at a height of 6". Leave 1½" of rail overhanging at each end to allow room for the addition of the crossbeams (see photo 1.1).

Once you have one side built, make a mirror image by flipping the first side so the rails are on the table and the posts are on top. Place your second set of posts on the first. Then line up the rails with the other side, making an evenly matched set. With both sides built, stabilize the sides by cross nailing all the joints (see photo 1.2).

1.1

1.2

2 Connecting the Sides

Connect the two sides with crossbeams measuring 18" long, 1½" diameter (see photo 2.1). Rest a crossbeam across the front of the two sides, and nail it into both posts so that good contact is made with the overlap of the rail. Driving the nail in at a slight angle will force the crossbeam downward into the rail (see photo 2.2). Alternate the nailing of crossbeams front and back to keep your frame square and aligned.

A total of nine crossbeams are to be added, two each for the top front, top back, bottom front, and bottom back (see photo 2.3). An additional beam is placed in the middle of the top rails to provide support for the seat railings to be installed later.

3 Nailing Intersecting Overlaps

Insert a nail wherever the rails and cross-beams overlap. This prevents the frame from swaying side to side. As always, the hole is pre-drilled, but in this case you are angling a nail into the end of the rail, an area that is susceptible to splitting. The pre-drilled hole should be at least as deep as the nail is long. You should also employ the old carpenter's trick of dulling the tip of the nail point. This lessens the likelihood of the nail point landing between the wood fibers and causing the log to crack and split.

4 Installing the Top Crossbeam

This top crossbeam will support the back of the sleigh, as well as create the junction where the handles will rest. It should be at least 21" long, with a 1½" diameter. Two nails should be cross nailed into the top of each back post. These nails should have their points dulled before being hammered home.

5 Creating a Cockpit

The seat area is surrounded by bent pieces that will form the sides of the sleigh. Starting 1" above the top side rail, nail the thick end of a bender to one of the back posts. Then, nail this bender to the front post, bend it around the front of the sleigh, and nail it to the front and back posts on the other side. Nail the thick end on alternate sides to balance the curves, spacing each bender about 1" apart. Four or five benders should be adequate. Make sure that the benders are fastened firmly in place. They will receive a lot of wear and tear as little people climb in and out of the sleigh.

6 Bending the Back

The thick end of the three benders that make up the round back are anchored on the inside of the top side rail (see photo 6.1). Nail the thick end on alternating sides to balance the curve. The first bender fits outside the side benders and is nailed into the back crossbeam as well as the top side rails (see photo 6.2). Nail the second and third benders to each other as well as the frame (see photo 6.3).

7 Installing the Handles

Handles are the next task. They are whittled to fit on top of the front legs (see photo 7.1), nailed down into the top of each leg (see photo 7.2), and up under the back crossbeam (see photo 7.3). Using dulled nails, double nail them in front of and into both the crossbeam and the leg in back. Leave the handles a little long in the back so they can be used for pushing and lifting.

8 Filling the Seat

The seat consists of eight ½" diameter pieces, each cut to a length that fits into the curved front. Nail the front of the sticks into the front crossbeams, leaving the back loose.

9 Filling in the Back

There are seven pieces in the back of the sleigh. Fit them in between the seat slats so that they extend below the seat. Nail the bottom of each slat into the front of the most forward rear crossbeam. (Access to this spot is easier if the sleigh is tipped on its back.) Fit the pieces in front of the top crossbeam, and nail them into the back of the three curved willow benders.

103

10 Reinforcing the Slats

Once all the slats are in position, go back and cross nail each joint in the back and in the seat.

11 Attaching the Rails

Attach the steel rails to the willow logs with three wood screws. These screws will need to be tightened occasionally. If they will no longer hold, replace them with a larger diameter screw.

12 Installing the Pull Rope

Tie 10' of rope around the bottom of the two front posts. For added effect, hang three little sleigh bells to a leather strap under the back crossbeam.

Birch Bark Canoe

This project can be built in a variety of sizes, to serve as either a decorative piece or as a functional vessel capable of navigating most waterways. In this particular instance, our canoe will be used to decorate the wall of a restaurant and is intended to look like an ancient artifact. For this reason we will purposely use bark that has holes in it and looks a little tattered. When finished, the canoe will be 8' long by 2' high and 18" across at its widest point.

8'

24" tall

18" at widest point

PROJECT REQUIREMENTS

4 peeled willow benders—
10' long, ¾" diameter

1 cedar board—
3' long, 6" wide, 1" thick

16 to 20 peeled willow rib benders—
3' long, ¾" diameter

peeled birch bark—
approximately 35 square feet

synthetic sinew—
1 large roll

silicone caulking to seal the seams
(or pine pitch for the true rustic experience)

1 Bending the Frame Pieces

Peel willow pieces to make the frame, using nice straight pieces no more than ¾" in diameter. Pieces about 10' long are used to make the side rails and the hull of the canoe. Once you have peeled ten long pieces, you must shape them and then secure them to a sheet of plywood where they can dry for a few days.

Four pieces are curved for the hull, and six are bent into a gentler curve to form the side rails. Drill screws halfway into a sheet of plywood in the shape that you want the sides and hull to take, then place the willows between the screws to dry in place. Remember that the exact shape and size of the hulls and side rails will vary according to the dimensions of the project. Because the wood takes a few days to dry, make a few extra pieces of each form to allow a little room for error or breakage.

Make sure these pieces are sheltered from any moisture and are exposed to ample air circulation. In a few days they will be quite dry and will retain the shape they were given. Remove them from the plywood and trim them to the exact length needed.

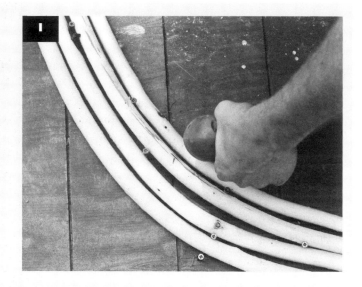

2 Connecting the Side Rails

Cut arrow-shaped blocks from 1" by 6"
cedar boards to connect the side rails and
form the top of the frame. Determine the
desired width, and then insert two 2" wide
cedar struts, cut to length, and placed at
equal distances from the ends. This will
stabilize the top of the frame and define
its shape.

3 Creating the Hull

The spine of the canoe is made up of two
bent pieces that are notched and fitted
together in the middle, ensuring that the two
ends of the canoe will be curved uniformly
(see photo 3.1). Drill a hole in each of the
arrow-shaped pieces connecting the ends
of the side rails. The hole should be large
enough for the thick end of a bender, or
approximately ¾" diameter (see photo 3.2).

Insert the thick end of a spine bender into
each of the holes and measure a notch 10"
long in the center of the two pieces. Cut the
notch so it matches what is shown in the
picture. Then, with the thick ends of the
benders secured in the arrow-shaped ends,
glue and screw the notches together
(see photo 3.3).

The first rib is then bent and attached to the hull at each strut, then secured with finishing nails. This will stabilize the structure and define the shape as the glue is allowed to set up (see photo 3.4).

4 Adding the Ribs

The ribs in our canoe will be placed 6" apart. The ribs must be individually fitted, then secured to plywood to dry overnight and allow them to shape, as was done with the side rails and hull. Once dry, they can be fastened with nails, and hammered into pre-drilled holes. Once the ribs are in place, the frame is finished.

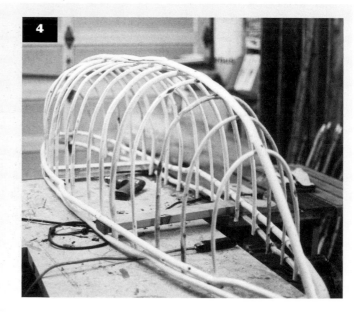

5 Peeling the Bark

Birch bark should be peeled during the summer months when the tree is actively growing. Make a vertical incision and gently pry the bark off, using a knife or a flat-edged scraper. The first layer should separate easily and peel off in a solid piece. (See "Peeling Birch Bark" in Chapter Four.)

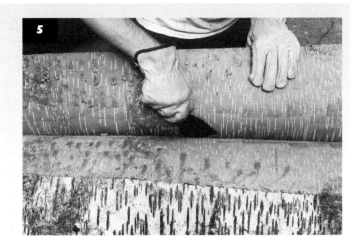

6 Attaching the Bark

A patchwork of birch bark will cover the frame, with synthetic sinew used as the thread that will hold the bark to the frame. Use a drill to make the holes for the sinew, which is threaded onto a heavy-duty needle; the drilled holes should be large enough for the threaded needle to fit through. The holes for the sinew should be drilled no more than 1" apart, and stitched in an X-pattern, as shown on the photo. As a general rule, the frame is covered starting from the ends and moving toward the middle (see photo 6.1).

Pieces of bark must be cut to custom fit over the ends of the frame. Custom cut one side of the end bark piece and then draw a mirror image on another piece of bark; sew the bottom edges together before attaching them to the frame (see photo 6.2). Continue wrapping pieces of bark around the frame, working from the ends to the middle. Once the frame is completely covered, trim off the excess bark (see photo 6.3).

Sealing seams in the birch bark is only necessary if the canoe is going to be functional. In that case, all seams should be glued with a waterproof adhesive, and sealed with silicone. Seams should run only vertically, and overlay each other from the front of the canoe to the back.

6.3

Rocking Chair

This beautiful rocking chair was made using traditional techniques. The dried wood frame is joined with handmade tenons, glued and allowed to dry while bound with rope. The matching curves of the back legs make the chair comfortable and allow it to rock easily without tipping back.

The design is full of small pieces that are layered on top of each other to create a woven flow of curves. This chair was designed by a customer who had a complete drawing, including all the relevant measurements. She rejected the first attempt and scrutinized the second very closely before deeming it worthy.

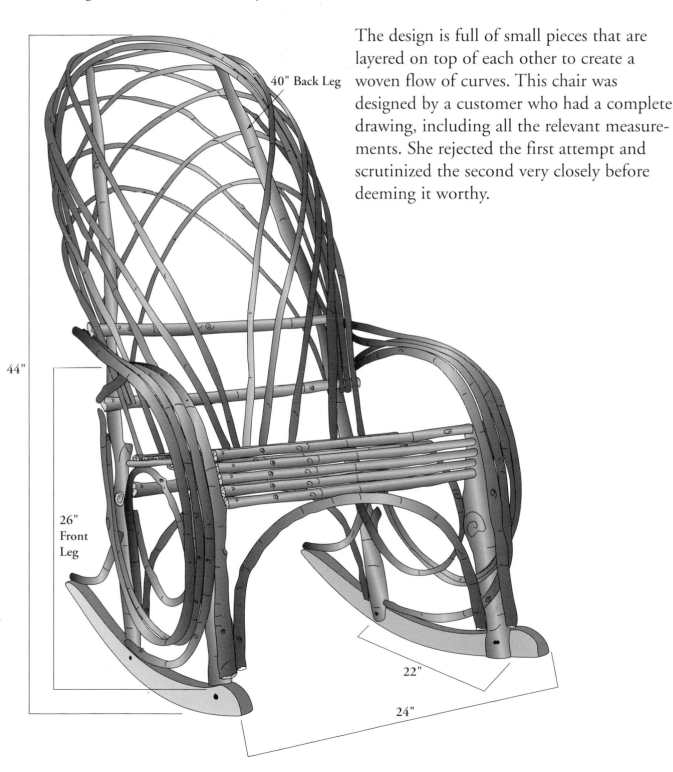

40" Back Leg

44"

26"
Front
Leg

22"

24"

PROJECT REQUIREMENTS

2 front legs—
15" long, 1½" diameter

2 rear legs—
40" long, 1½" diameter

4 side rails—
18" long, 1" diameter

4 crossbeams—
20" long, 1" diameter

2 arm anchors—
26" long, 1½" diameter

1 willow back bender—
45" long, ¾" diameter (very straight)

8 arm benders—
5' long, ¾" diameter

8 back benders—
4' long, ¾" diameter

8 back fill benders—
5' long, ½" diameter

2 front seat blocks—
1½" long, ¾" diameter

1 middle seat support—
20" long, 1" diameter

25 to 30 seat slats—
½" diameter, length cut to size
(approx. 21")

2 maple pieces for rockers—
40" long, 6" wide, 1" thick

4 carriage bolts and nuts—
3" long, ¼" diameter

1 Building the Sides

Each side consists of: a 15" long,
1½" diameter front leg; a 40" long,
1½" diameter rear leg; and two 18" long,
1½" diameter side rails. (Photo 2 clearly
shows the curve needed on the rear
legs to support the seat back.)

Drill a ¾" mortise at 3" and 13" from the
bottom of each leg. Each tenon on the side
rails is hand cut and fit into the mortise on
the legs. The two top side rails must be
straight and have a level edge along the top,
because they will support the seat.

Once both sides are cut, fitted, and matched,
apply glue to both surfaces of the joints.
Then tie two ropes around each joint, bind
the joints as tightly as possible, and leave
them to dry overnight. (See Chapter Four,
"Fitting the Joints," for more details on tying
and drying joints.)

2 Connecting the Sides

To connect the sides of the frame, fit four 20" crossbeams into mortises placed at 4" and 14" from the bottom of each of the legs. Glue the joints and tie with rope, making sure that even pressure is applied to the eight joints. It is important that the frame remains square and centered.

Allow the frame to sit for a few days. The glue must be dry before proceeding.

113

3 Installing Arm Anchors

Install two 26" long, 1½" diameter arm anchors across the back legs at 22" and 26" from the bottom of the frame. Double nail them into the back legs.

4 Installing the Main Back Loop

A single bender will define the shape of the chair back. We are using a premium piece, measuring 45" long, ¾" diameter. Shape the bender into a nice curve, and anchor it securely into the legs, the arm anchors, and the inside of the side rails.

5 Making the Horseshoe Loops

The back of the chair is filled in by three layers, with the first two completed in this step.

The first layer consists of four loops that resemble lopsided horseshoes. Start the first loop on the inside of the back leg, just above the seat. Loop it to the other side and nail it onto the inside of the other back leg (see photo 5.1). Add three more loops to the same side; each should start a few inches above the last and follow the same shape, but always finish in the same place on the inside of the back leg.

The second layer is the mirror image of the first. Add four loops to this layer, for a total of eight loops filling in the back (see photo 5.2).

114

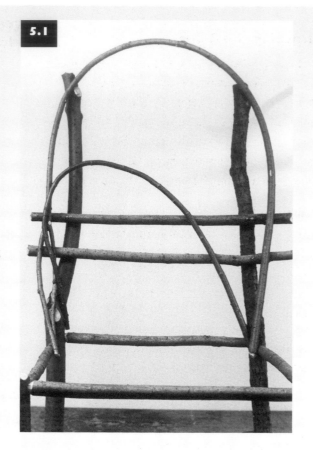

5.1

5.2

6 Attaching the Arms

Nail the thin end of the first arm piece into the front surface of the front leg. Bend it back in an arch, and then nail it into the lower arm anchor (see photo 6.1). The maximum height of the arch should be 26" from the floor. Attach the arm on the other side and adjust the height until the arms are even.

Nail the thick end of the second arm piece into the lower arm anchor and follow the path of the first arm piece. Nail the bender into the first arm piece, loop the thin end around, and nail it into the back leg (see photo 6.2).

Start the next two arm pieces from the upper arm anchor. Follow the arch of the first two pieces and end up by curving the thin ends up the back leg. As you attach these benders, nail each one into the previous arm piece (see photo 6.2).

6.1

6.2

7 Completing the Back

Eight more pieces are added to complete the third layer of fill in the seat back. Start with the thick end of a bender and nail it into the upper back crossbeam. Run the piece in a shallow arch up to the top of the back, then bend the piece around to the back of the chair and wind it around the main back loop (see photo 7.1). Add three more pieces to this side, working from the middle to the outside.

When the first side is complete, add four matching pieces to the other side to finish filling in the seat back (see photo 7.2).

7.1

7.2

8 Adding Seat Supports

Three seat supports are required before the seat can be built. First, fit two blocks, each 1½" long, just below seat level on the inside of the front legs (see photo 8.1). Attach them to the front legs with three nails, pre-drilling the nail holes to avoid splitting the small blocks. (Shave the side of the block to get a better fit against the leg.)

Second, fit a middle seat support under the front and rear top crossbeams, along the mid-line of the seat (see photo 8.2). This rail should be 18" long, ¾" diameter. The support should be below the front top crossbeam so that it will not interfere with the pieces that will be added later to the underside of the front seat.

117

9 Building the Seat

Fill in the seat with ½" diameter pieces cut to fit across the side rails and middle support. Start at the front of the chair and fit the first piece inside the front legs, with the ends supported by the blocks you just installed. Cut the ends of the first piece at an angle so it fits snugly against the front legs (see photo 9.1). Double nail the piece into the middle seat support and nail the ends into the legs. Don't nail the ends into the blocks or they could split.

Add more pieces and work toward the back of the seat, double nailing into the middle support and nailing once into the side rails (see photo 9.2). Alternate which side you put the thick end of the pieces to keep the seat square. Use straight pieces of a similar diameter to ensure that the seat is level and comfortable. Build about three-quarters of the seat, and then work from the back, meeting somewhere in the middle.

10 Filling in the Front

Fill in the front of the seat using pieces that fit just under the top front crossbeam and hide the middle seat support. Use the blocks on the inside of the front legs for support only. Nail the ends of the pieces into the front legs, and double nail them into the end of the middle seat support. Make sure you pre-drill all holes when building log furniture, especially when nailing into the ends of logs.

11 Affixing Decorative Loops

Install a few decorative loops front and back, nailing them firmly into the legs. You can get as carried away as you like, but I maintain a general rule of keeping ornamentation as simple as possible.

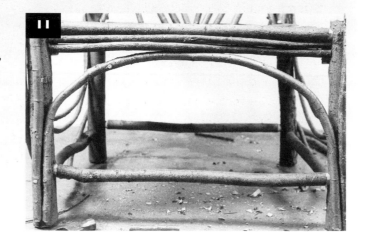

12 Making the Rockers

The rockers are more work than you might think. Using a cardboard template, trace the rocker shape onto a piece of 1" by 6" hardwood (maple in this project), then cut the rocker. This template was made by copying the rocker of an existing chair and then adapting it to suit my needs.

Sand and stain the rockers, then let them sit to dry.

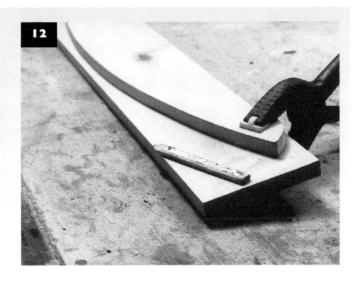

13 Installing the Rockers

Lay the chair on its side and position one of the rockers against the outside bottom of the front and back legs. The rocker should extend about 3" beyond the front and rear legs. On each of the four chair legs, mark the spot where you will attach the rocker, making sure the rocker will always be in contact with the floor. Cut halfway through the bottom of each leg at that point to create a notch where the rocker will fit into the leg (see photo 13.1).

Drill a pilot hole in the marked positions on the legs and the rocker. Then, drill holes through the rocker and the legs a bit larger in diameter than the shaft of the bolt you will use. Fasten the rocker to the legs with carriage bolts (see photo 13.2).

Flip the chair on its other side and repeat the process to attach the second rocker.

Trim the bolts and paint them so that they are less visible.

Mosaic-top Coffee Table

This coffee table has a beautiful mosaic top made of ceramic tile in a fleur-de-lis design. This particular top was designed by a mosaic artist at Destina Inc., in Edmonton, Alberta, but you can do the work yourself, or find an artisan in your neck of the woods who can design one for you. The table is designed for an exterior application, so we are using porcelain tiles that will not absorb moisture and an exterior mortar that will allow for some expansion and contraction of the wood.

The simple mortise and tenon base can be altered to make a nice dining table. The base must have a sturdy construction to match the visual weight of the top, as well as to support its mass.

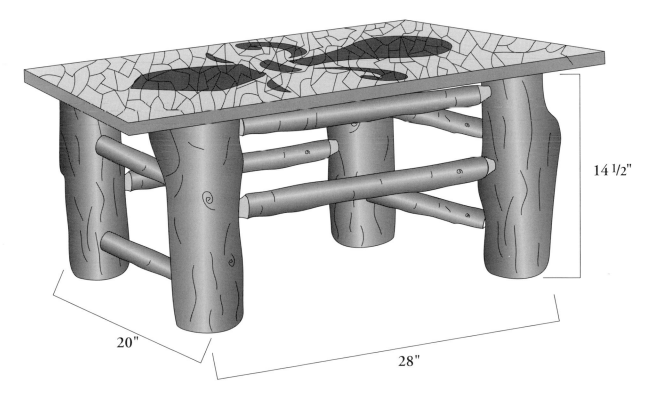

14 1/2"

20"

28"

PROJECT REQUIREMENTS

4 table legs—
14½" long, 5" diameter

4 side rails—
20" long, 1½" diameter

4 crossbeams—
28" long, 1½" diameter

2 plywood pieces for top—
48" long, 32" wide, ¾" thick

porcelain tile—
approx. 12 square feet

exterior mortar

grout

grout sealant

1 Making the Sides for the Base

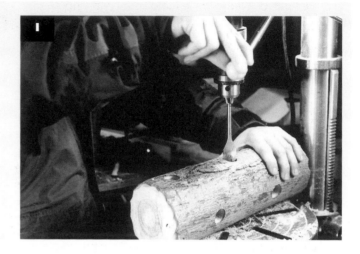

Each side of the base consists of: two 14½" long, 5" diameter legs; and two 20" long, 1½" diameter side rails. As with all tables, make sure the four legs are the same length so that your tabletop is level in the end.

Whittle the rough edges of two of the legs, then drill pilot holes for mortises at 2" and 7" from the top. Drill the two mortises 1½" deep, using a paddle bit with a 1" diameter.

Cut a 1" tenon on each end of the side rails and fit the two legs and two side rails together, trimming where necessary to make things square.

Build the other side to match the first side.

2 Gluing the Sides Together

Once you are satisfied with the fit of each side, remove the legs and drill a pilot hole through each mortise to the outside of the log. (If you don't have a drill bit that is long enough, try using a long wood screw.) Drill a countersink hole from the outside. Apply glue to both the tenon and mortise, then fit each side back together. Use a rubber mallet to ensure a good fit.

Pull the joint together by inserting a long wood screw into the countersink channel and tightening it.

3 Connecting the Base

The two sides are connected by four 28" long, 1½" diameter crossbeams. On the inside of each leg, drill pilot holes for the mortise at 4" and 10" from the top. Drill the mortise 1½" deep, using a 1" paddle bit.

Make a 1" tenon on each end of the four crossbeams, then fit the crossbeams into the legs. Trim where necessary to get a square fit.

Glue and screw the joints, just as you did in step 2.

4 Preparing the Top

Two pieces of ¾" plywood, 32" wide by 48" long, are used for the tabletop. Screw the two pieces together, for a total thickness of 1½". Seal the plywood with a sanding sealer to help resist moisture.

123

5 Edging the Top

Cut tiles into 1" strips to surround the table edge on all four sides. Attach these side pieces with mortar, ensuring they are level with the top of the table.

6 Mortaring the Tiles

The pattern for this table is a green fleur-de-lis on an off-white background, but the design possibilities are limited only by your imagination. Break the porcelain tiles with a hammer, then assemble them to make the design and the background. This pattern was first made on a plastic mesh and then laid down on the board, but you can skip this step by drawing the design outline directly onto the plywood tabletop.

Cover the design area with a ¼" film of exterior mortar (see photo 6.1). (Note: Only mortar as much area as you can fill in a 10-minute period because the mortar is designed to set up quickly.) Fill the design area with pieces of green tile (see photo 6.2). Once the design is finished, start filling the surrounding area with the background color (see photo 6.3).

Your surface tiles should overlap the 1" edge pieces. By using the tiles' natural edges, you can make a smooth outside edge on all sides of the tabletop.

Let the mortar dry for 48 hours before applying the grout.

124

7 Grouting the Top

Grout must be applied to fill the spaces between the tiles and to make the surface even.

Mix the grout according to the manufacturer's instructions and apply it to all surfaces, including the edges (see photo 7.1). Smooth the surface with your hands, liberally filling in all the spaces (see photo 7.2).

Immediately after applying the grout, wipe all surfaces with a damp sponge to wash away the excess grout (see photo 7.3). Make sure that you don't remove too much grout and that the surface remains level. Let the grout dry for 20 minutes and then wipe the tiles with a dry cloth to remove any residue.

7.1

7.2

7.3

8 Sealing the Grout

Let the grout dry for ten to fifteen days before sealing the surface of the grout. Apply a liquid exterior grout sealant (available from a tile supply store) to the grout only and allow it to dry.

9 Connecting the Top and the Base

Flip the top upside down and position the base upside down on it, making sure the base is centered. Attach small blocks of wood to the insides of the legs and then screw them to the underside of the tabletop. Make sure to pre-drill holes through the blocks so that the wood will not split.

Candle Holder

This simple project uses some of those little bits that are left over from larger projects. A variety of candle holders of different heights and diameters can be made, and larger diameter logs can hold more than one candle. To minimize the risk of fire, it is best to use a pan candle that has a metal lining. A regular candle can be used, but there must be a layer of non-flammable insulation between the candle and the wood. Remember to put safety first.

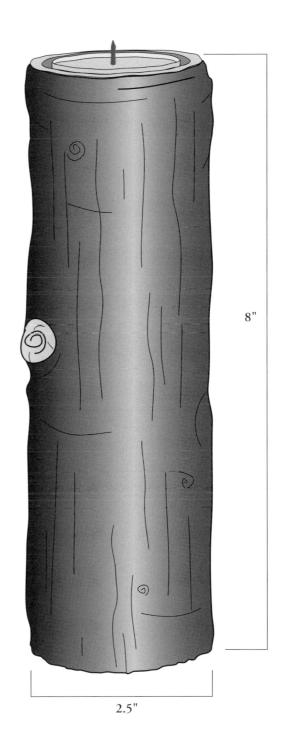

8"

2.5"

PROJECT REQUIREMENTS

1 piece of log—
  length and thickness can vary to suit the design

1 Squaring the Block

Make sure that the log you've chosen sits flat and has a level surface for the candle to sit in. For this project, we have squared the end of a longer log, and then cut an 8" piece.

2 Pre-drilling a Hole

Pre-drill a pilot hole in the top of the log in the center of where the candle will sit. In this project, the hole is in the middle of the log, but it could be offset or multiple holes could be drilled in a larger log.

3 Drilling a Candle Pan Hole

The candle pan is ½" deep, 1½" diameter. Wrap the log in an old towel or a piece of leather to protect the bark, then secure it in a vise. With a 1⅜" paddle bit, drill a hole to a depth of slightly more than ½".

4 Finishing the Edges

The edges of the log should be cleaned up, as should the lip of the candle pan hole. Use a utility knife to whittle the edges of the log. Place the blade at a 45-degree angle and make a cut. Start your next cut at the edge of the first cut, and continue making crescent-shaped cuts around the log. For the inside edge of the hole, simply run the blade around the edge and smooth any rough fibers.

5 Fitting the Candle

The candle should sit nicely in the hole. Make sure the candle is level and stable so that it will burn safely.

129

CONVERSION TABLE

All measurements in this book use imperial measurements, because imperial units are the standard for the construction industry. However, for those people more comfortable using metric units, the following tables are designed to give you a guide to make the necessary conversions.

IMPERIAL MEASUREMENT	METRIC EQUIVALENT
1 inch	2.54 centimeters
½" inch	1.27 centimeters
¾" inch	1.91 centimeters
12 inches (1 foot)	30.48 centimeters (0.305 meters)
1 foot (12 inches)	0.305 meters (30.48 centimeters)

METRIC MEASUREMENT	IMPERIAL EQUIVALENT
1 centimeter	approx. $^{13}/_{32}$ inch
½ centimeter (5 millimeters)	approx. $^{3}/_{16}$ inch
¾ centimeter (7.5 millimeters)	approx. $^{5}/_{16}$ inch
1 decimeter (10 centimeters)	approx. 3 $^{15}/_{16}$ inches
1 meter (100 centimeters)	approx. 3 feet, 3 ⅜ inch (39 ⅜ inches)

FOR QUICK CONVERSION:

MULTIPLY	BY	OR DIVIDE	BY	TO OBTAIN
centimeters	0.39	centimeters	2.54	inches
feet	0.31	feet	3.28	meters
inches	2.54	inches	0.39	centimeters
meters	3.28	meters	0.31	feet

GLOSSARY OF TERMS

bender
See "willow bender."

bow saw
A small saw with a cross-cut blade used for cutting or pruning small trees.

cleat
A hidden bracket that connects two or more parts of a piece of furniture.

coppice wood
The undergrowth of hardwood trees.

countersink bit
A cone-shaped drill bit used for cutting center channels. Used to recess screw heads.

crossbeam
A frame element that runs perpendicular to the mid-line of a piece of furniture.

cross nailing
Installing two nails at opposing angles in the same spot.

galvanized
Coated with zinc to prevent oxidation; process is applied to metal.

hole saw
Rotary cutting blade that cuts a circle. Used on the end of a power drill.

joint
A connecting point between two or more furniture parts.

linseed oil
An oil produced from flax seed. Used to protect furniture from sustaining water damage.

mortise
Half of a joint, made of a hole into which a wooden peg (tenon) is inserted.

nail set
A long, cylindrical tool used to drive nails into hard-to-access places.

paddle bit
A paddle-shaped drill bit used for making holes.

peeled wood
Material with bark removed.

plug cutter
A rotary cutting tool that cuts wood plugs to fit specified diameters.

pneumatic tool
An implement that shoots fasteners (nails or staples) using a stream of pressurized air.

pre-drilling
Creating a channel in the wood to guide a fastener, such as a nail or screw.

pruning shears
A hand tool with a cutting blade that closes onto an anvil.

router
A rotary cutting tool that accepts a variety of bits. Used for cutting grooves or shaping wood.

seat slats
Long, thin pieces of wood used to fill the seat of a chair or bench.

side rail
Frame element that runs parallel to the mid-line of a piece of furniture.

spar varnish
A sealant used to protect wood used in marine applications.

tenon
Half of a joint, made of a peg or shaft that fits into a hole (mortise).

utility knife
A simple, metal knife with a replaceable blade.

UV-blocking agent
Chemical filter that reflects ultraviolet light and prevents wood from sustaining sun damage.

whittling
General trimming of wood with a knife to shape it to match needs or smooth rough edges.

willow bender
A long, straight willow shoot used to make curves.

Notes to Self

Please feel free to use these pages to try new design ideas, or to remind yourself of the tricks and shortcuts you've learned while working on the projects in this book.

133

OTHER FIFTH HOUSE BOOKS YOU WILL ENJOY

PERFECT PARTNERS
Beautiful Plant Combinations for Prairie Gardens
By Liesbeth Leatherbarrow and Lesley Reynolds

$24.95 paperback; 208 pages
ISBN: 1-894004-78-7

Create a beautiful garden by learning which plants look good and grow well together. *Perfect Partners* is packed with great plant suggestions, lists of flowering times, plants sizes, growing tips, soil requirements, color photographs, and more.

THE PRAIRIE GARDENER'S SOURCEBOOK
A Guide to Finding the Best Plants, Seeds, Products, and Information for Your Garden
By June Flanagan and Donna Fremont

$16.95 paperback; 224 pages
ISBN: 1-894004-66-3

An indispensable resource for cold-climate gardeners, this book is filled with information on seeds, plants, horticultural societies, garden products, public gardens, help lines, recommended publications, and more.

BEST BULBS FOR THE PRAIRIES
By Liesbeth Leatherbarrow and Lesley Reynolds

$19.95 paperback; 192 pages
ISBN: 1-894004-61-2

Add color, texture, and interest to your prairie garden with spring, summer, and fall blooming bulbs. Color photographs, landscaping tips, naturalizing and fertilizing information, and dozens of hardy and tender bulbs make this book a must-have.

101 BEST PLANTS FOR THE PRAIRIES
By Liesbeth Leatherbarrow and Lesley Reynolds

$19.95 paperback; 264 pages
ISBN: 1-894004-30-2

Take the guesswork out of gardening with this guide to the best perennials, annuals, bulbs, shrubs, and trees for the prairies. Filled with detailed growing information, color and bloom charts, and beautiful color photographs.

Look for these books at quality bookstores and garden centers, or order directly by calling: 1-800-387-9776.